The Wellness Plate

Delicious Recipes and Tips for a Healthier You

Sophia Bennett

The Wellness Plate

Table of Contents

Chapter 1: Building the Foundation of Wellness

Understanding Nutritional Essentials

Understanding nutritional essentials involves unraveling the intricate tapestry of nutrients that fuel the body. It requires delving into the components that provide energy, support growth, and maintain optimal health. Each nutrient plays a unique role, and understanding these can empower individuals to make informed food choices that contribute to their overall well-being.

Nutrients can be broadly categorized into macronutrients and micronutrients. Macronutrients consist of carbohydrates, proteins, and fats, which are required in larger quantities. They are the primary energy sources and building blocks for the body. Carbohydrates are the body's preferred energy source, breaking down into glucose to fuel bodily functions. They can be found in whole grains, fruits, and vegetables. Proteins, made up of amino acids, are essential for tissue repair, immune function, and muscle growth. They are present in foods like meat, fish, beans, and legumes. Fats, often misunderstood, are vital for brain function, hormone production, and nutrient absorption. Healthy fats, such as those found in avocados, nuts, and olive oil, should be included in a balanced diet.

Micronutrients, on the other hand, are vitamins and minerals needed in smaller amounts but are equally crucial. They support a wide range of physiological functions, from bone health to immune response. Vitamins like A, C, and E act as antioxidants, combating oxidative stress and supporting skin health. B vitamins are vital for energy metabolism and brain function.

Minerals such as calcium and magnesium are essential for bone strength and muscle function, whereas iron is crucial for oxygen transport in the blood.

Hydration is another fundamental aspect often overlooked in discussions of nutrition. Water makes up a significant portion of the human body and is involved in nearly every physiological process. Staying hydrated aids digestion, regulates body temperature, and supports cognitive function. While individual water needs vary, a general guideline is to drink enough fluids to maintain clear urine and ensure adequate hydration throughout the day.

The balance between macronutrients and micronutrients is a delicate dance that varies based on individual needs, lifestyle, and health goals. For example, an athlete may require more carbohydrates for energy, while someone looking to build muscle might focus on protein intake. Understanding the body's unique requirements is key to tailoring a nutrition plan that supports one's lifestyle.

Fresh ingredients play a pivotal role in the nutrient density of meals. Whole, unprocessed foods retain their natural nutrients, providing a more potent nutritional punch. For instance, choosing whole fruits over fruit juices ensures fiber intake, which aids digestion and keeps hunger at bay. Fresh vegetables, when consumed in a variety, offer a spectrum of vitamins and minerals vital for health. Incorporating seasonal produce not only supports local agriculture but also maximizes nutrient intake, as these foods are harvested at their nutritional peak.

Cooking at home offers the opportunity to control the ingredients and cooking methods, preserving the nutritional integrity of meals. Homemade meals allow for the use of healthy cooking oils, controlled salt, and sugar levels, and the inclusion of a variety of nutrient-rich foods. The act of cooking also fosters a deeper connection to the food, leading to more mindful eating practices and a greater appreciation for the nourishment it provides.

Stocking a kitchen with healthful staples is a foundational step toward maintaining a nutritious diet. Pantry essentials such as whole grains, legumes, nuts, and seeds can form the base of countless meals. Fresh produce, lean proteins, and dairy or dairy alternatives should be part of regular grocery lists. Having a variety of herbs and spices on hand not only enhances flavor but also adds an array of antioxidants and anti-inflammatory properties to dishes.

It's important to acknowledge the role of cultural and personal preferences in shaping dietary choices. Food is deeply intertwined with tradition and identity, and understanding nutrition doesn't mean abandoning cherished culinary practices. Instead, it emphasizes the integration of these practices with nutritional knowledge to create a balanced and fulfilling diet. For instance, traditional dishes can be adapted to include more fresh vegetables or lean proteins, aligning them with modern nutritional insights while preserving cultural heritage.

Navigating the world of nutrition can be overwhelming, with trends and fad diets often muddying the waters. It's crucial to approach nutrition with a critical mindset, focusing on evidence-based practices rather than fleeting dietary trends. Consulting with nutritionists or healthcare providers can provide personalized guidance and support.

Mindful eating is a practice that encourages awareness of hunger cues, food choices, and eating habits. It involves paying attention to the sensory experiences of eating, such as taste, texture, and aroma, leading to a more satisfying and nourishing experience. By fostering a positive relationship with food, mindful eating can reduce overeating and enhance overall enjoyment of meals.

Understanding nutritional essentials is not a one-size-fits-all approach. It is a dynamic process that evolves with the individual's life stage, health status, and personal goals. Embracing this journey with curiosity and openness can lead to a more balanced, vibrant, and healthful life.

Balancing Flavors and Nutrients

Balancing flavors and nutrients is an art that transforms everyday meals into culinary masterpieces that delight the palate and nourish the body. Imagine a dinner plate as a symphony, where each ingredient plays its part in harmony, creating a sensory experience that satisfies both taste and nutritional needs. Achieving this balance requires an understanding of how to combine different flavors—sweet, salty, sour, bitter, and umami—with the essential nutrients that support health.

Begin by exploring the world of flavor profiles. Sweetness, often found in fruits, honey, and certain vegetables like carrots and sweet potatoes, can create a sense of indulgence and comfort. It pairs beautifully with the acidity of sour flavors, such as citrus fruits, vinegar, and fermented foods, which add brightness and zest. Salt enhances the natural taste of ingredients, acting as a flavor amplifier without overpowering. Think of how a pinch of salt can transform a bland dish into something vibrant. Bitter elements, such as dark leafy greens, coffee, and certain herbs, bring complexity and depth. Finally, umami, the savory essence found in mushrooms, tomatoes, aged cheeses, and soy sauce, adds richness and body, rounding out the flavor spectrum.

When crafting a meal, consider how these flavors interact. A salad with arugula (bitter), cherry tomatoes (sweet), feta cheese (salty), and a balsamic vinaigrette (sour and umami) creates a delightful balance that excites the senses. Similarly, a stir-fry featuring broccoli (bitter), bell peppers (sweet), soy sauce (salty and umami), and a squeeze of lime (sour) can offer a satisfying and nutritious experience.

Beyond flavor, the balance of nutrients is crucial for a meal that supports overall well-being. Carbohydrates provide energy, and incorporating whole grains like quinoa, brown rice, or barley ensures a steady release of energy while adding texture and substance. Proteins are the building blocks of the body, essential for muscle repair and growth. Including a variety of protein sources, such as lean meats, beans, tofu, or lentils, not only caters to different dietary preferences but also introduces diverse flavors and textures.

Fats, often misunderstood, are vital for brain health and the absorption of fat-soluble vitamins. Healthy fats found in avocados, nuts, seeds, and olive oil contribute creaminess and richness to dishes. Picture a creamy avocado dressing draped over a vibrant salad, adding both flavor and a nutrient boost. Micronutrients, though required in smaller amounts, play significant roles in maintaining health. Fruits and vegetables, with their vivid colors, are rich sources of vitamins and minerals. A plate brimming with a rainbow of produce not only appeals visually but also ensures a broad spectrum of nutrients.

The preparation of ingredients can significantly impact both flavor and nutritional quality. Cooking methods like grilling, roasting, and steaming preserve nutrients while enhancing natural flavors. Roasting vegetables, for instance, caramelizes their natural sugars, deepening their sweetness and adding complexity. Steaming retains the vibrant color and crispness of vegetables, maintaining their nutritional integrity.

Herbs and spices are the secret weapons of flavor balancing, offering endless possibilities without adding extra calories or sodium. Fresh herbs like basil, cilantro, and mint introduce bright, aromatic notes, while spices such as cumin, turmeric, and paprika add warmth and depth. Experimenting with different combinations can transform a simple dish into a memorable culinary experience. Consider a roasted vegetable medley seasoned with rosemary and thyme or a grilled chicken breast marinated with cumin and coriander for a burst of flavor.

Mindful eating practices enhance the enjoyment and appreciation of balanced meals. Taking the time to savor each bite, recognizing the interplay of flavors and textures, can lead to a more satisfying dining experience. This mindfulness extends to portion sizes, where listening to hunger cues helps prevent overeating and promotes a healthier relationship with food.

Cultural and personal preferences also play a vital role in balancing flavors and nutrients. Food is deeply intertwined with tradition and identity, and accommodating these aspects enriches the dining experience. Acknowledging these preferences while incorporating nutritional balance allows for a more inclusive and enjoyable meal. For example, a traditional pasta dish can be enhanced with a variety of vegetables and lean proteins, creating a balanced meal that respects culinary heritage.

The balance of flavors and nutrients is not a rigid formula but a flexible approach that adapts to individual tastes and dietary needs. It encourages creativity and exploration, inviting individuals to experiment with new ingredients and cooking techniques. By embracing this dynamic process, meals become more than sustenance; they become an expression of personal style and a celebration of the senses.

Ultimately, the journey of balancing flavors and nutrients is about creating harmony on the plate and in the body. It is a holistic approach that nourishes both physically and emotionally, fostering a deeper connection to the food we eat and the way it supports our health. By mastering this art, individuals can enjoy meals that are not only delicious but also contribute to a vibrant, balanced lifestyle.

The Role of Fresh Ingredients

The role of fresh ingredients in our diets is both profound and transformative, offering a multitude of benefits that extend far beyond mere nutrition. Picture a vibrant farmer's market, brimming with an array of colorful fruits, crisp vegetables, aromatic herbs, and freshly baked goods. Each item tells a story of its journey from earth to table, promising flavors and nutrients that processed foods simply cannot match.

Fresh ingredients are the foundation of a nutritious diet. They are often richer in essential vitamins and minerals compared to their processed counterparts. This is due to their minimal exposure to heat, light, and air—elements that can degrade nutrients during processing and storage. For example, a fresh tomato picked at the peak of ripeness offers a potent dose of vitamin C and lycopene, antioxidants that support immune function and reduce the risk of chronic diseases. Similarly, leafy greens such as spinach and kale provide abundant iron and folate, crucial for energy production and cell growth.

Beyond nutritional value, fresh ingredients enhance the sensory experience of eating. The crisp snap of a freshly harvested carrot, the juicy burst of a ripe strawberry, and the fragrant aroma of freshly picked basil all contribute to a more enjoyable and satisfying meal. These sensory delights encourage mindful eating, where attention is paid to the flavors, textures, and aromas of the meal, promoting a deeper appreciation for the food and its role in nourishing the body.

The journey of fresh ingredients often begins with sustainable farming practices. Local farms, which prioritize soil health and biodiversity, produce food that is both environmentally friendly and nutritionally superior. Supporting local agriculture not only ensures fresher produce but also reduces the carbon footprint associated with long-distance food transportation. This symbiotic relationship between consumers and local farmers fosters a sense of community and connection to the land, enhancing the overall dining experience.

Incorporating fresh ingredients into daily meals requires a bit of planning and creativity. A well-stocked pantry and a weekly meal plan can make all the difference. Begin by selecting a variety of seasonal produce, which is often more affordable and flavorful. Seasonal foods are harvested at their peak, ensuring optimal taste and nutritional content. For instance, summer berries burst with sweetness, while winter squash offers comforting earthiness.

Preparation methods can greatly impact the flavor and nutritional quality of fresh ingredients. Simple techniques such as steaming, roasting, and grilling preserve nutrients while enhancing natural flavors. A quick steam of broccoli retains its vibrant color and crispness, while roasting root vegetables caramelizes their natural sugars, deepening their sweetness. Grilling adds a smoky depth to meats and vegetables, creating complex flavors with minimal added fats.

Fresh herbs and spices are invaluable in elevating dishes, providing a burst of flavor without relying on excessive salt or sugar. Imagine a sprinkle of freshly chopped cilantro over a spicy curry or a handful of basil leaves stirred into a tomato sauce. These additions not only enhance taste but also offer their own nutritional benefits. Herbs like parsley and thyme boast anti-inflammatory and antioxidant properties, contributing to overall health.

The versatility of fresh ingredients allows for endless culinary exploration. A single ingredient can be transformed into numerous dishes, each highlighting a different aspect of its flavor profile. Take tomatoes, for instance; they can be sliced into a caprese salad, simmered into a rich marinara sauce, or blended into a refreshing gazpacho. This adaptability encourages creativity in the kitchen and helps prevent meal monotony.

For those new to cooking with fresh ingredients, start small and gradually expand your repertoire. Experiment with new produce or unfamiliar herbs, integrating them into familiar recipes to build confidence and experience. Perhaps try adding a handful of arugula to a pasta dish for a peppery kick, or incorporate roasted beets into a salad for an earthy sweetness.

Accessibility is key when it comes to fresh ingredients. Community-supported agriculture (CSA) programs and farmer's markets offer convenient options for sourcing local produce. Many grocery stores now prioritize fresh and organic sections, making it easier than ever to find quality ingredients. Additionally, growing your own herbs or vegetables, even in small spaces, can provide a rewarding and sustainable source of fresh produce.

The benefits of fresh ingredients extend beyond the individual, impacting broader societal and environmental factors. By choosing fresh and local foods, we support sustainable agriculture, reduce food waste, and promote biodiversity. This collective effort contributes to a healthier planet and a more resilient food system.

Ultimately, the role of fresh ingredients in our diets is multifaceted, touching on aspects of nutrition, flavor, sustainability, and community. By embracing fresh ingredients, we open ourselves to a world of culinary possibilities that enrich our meals and our lives. This journey is not just about consuming food; it's about fostering a deeper connection to what we eat, where it comes from, and how it supports our health and well-being.

The Benefits of Cooking at Home

Cooking at home offers an abundance of benefits that extend beyond the immediate satisfaction of a delicious meal. It is an empowering practice that not only nurtures the body but also enriches the mind and soul. Imagine the aroma of freshly baked bread wafting through the kitchen, the sizzle of vegetables in a hot pan, and the vibrant colors of a well-composed plate. These sensory experiences are just the beginning of the journey toward a healthier, more fulfilling lifestyle.

One of the most significant advantages of cooking at home is the control it affords over ingredients. In an era where processed foods dominate the market, knowing exactly what goes into your meals is a powerful tool for health. Home cooking allows for the selection of fresh, whole ingredients, free from the additives and preservatives often found in pre-packaged foods. This control extends to the choice of cooking methods, enabling the preparation of meals with minimal added fats, sugars, and sodium.

Cooking at home encourages a more balanced diet, as it allows for the incorporation of a wide variety of food groups. Whole grains, lean proteins, fresh vegetables, and healthy fats can be combined in myriad ways to create nutritious and satisfying dishes. This diversity not only pleases the palate but also ensures a comprehensive intake of essential nutrients, supporting overall health and well-being.

Financially, cooking at home is often more economical than dining out or relying on convenience foods. With a bit of planning, meals can be prepared in advance, reducing the temptation for costly takeout. Buying ingredients in bulk, focusing on seasonal produce, and minimizing food waste are strategies that further enhance the cost-effectiveness of home cooking. The money saved can be redirected toward other priorities, contributing to financial stability.

The process of cooking fosters creativity and personal expression. Each meal becomes an opportunity to experiment with different flavors, textures, and cuisines. Whether it's trying a new spice blend, adapting a recipe to personal taste, or inventing a dish from scratch, the kitchen becomes a canvas for culinary exploration. This creative outlet can be both fulfilling and therapeutic, providing a sense of accomplishment and joy.

Cooking at home also strengthens family bonds and social connections. Preparing and sharing meals with loved ones creates a space for communication and togetherness. The act of cooking together, whether with family or friends, encourages collaboration and fosters a sense of shared purpose. These moments around the kitchen table can lead to cherished memories and deepen relationships.

Mindfulness is another benefit that comes with home cooking. Engaging in the preparation of food encourages a focus on the present moment, a mindfulness practice that can reduce stress and enhance mental clarity. This mindfulness extends to eating, where savoring each bite and appreciating the flavors and textures leads to a more satisfying dining experience.

Safety and health considerations are also paramount. Home cooking allows for the implementation of food safety practices, reducing the risk of foodborne illnesses. Proper handling, cooking, and storage of ingredients are easier to manage at home, ensuring meals are not only delicious but also safe to consume.

For those with dietary restrictions or preferences, cooking at home provides the flexibility to tailor meals to specific needs. Whether it's accommodating allergies, following a plant-based diet, or managing health conditions, home cooking allows for the customization of recipes to suit individual requirements. This personalization ensures that dietary goals are met without sacrificing taste or enjoyment.

The skills gained from home cooking are invaluable and lifelong. Learning to prepare meals cultivates a sense of self-sufficiency and confidence in the kitchen. As these skills develop, cooking becomes more efficient and enjoyable, transforming from a chore into a rewarding practice. This expertise can be shared with others, passing on knowledge and inspiring future generations to embrace the benefits of home cooking.

The environmental impact of home cooking is another consideration. By choosing local and sustainable ingredients, reducing food waste, and minimizing packaging, home cooks can contribute to a more sustainable food system. This conscious approach not only benefits the planet but also aligns with a lifestyle that values health, well-being, and responsibility.

Ultimately, the benefits of cooking at home are as diverse as they are profound. It is a practice that nourishes the body, nurtures the mind, and enriches the spirit. By embracing the art of home cooking, individuals embark on a journey toward a healthier, more connected, and fulfilling life, one meal at a time.

Stocking Your Kitchen for Health

Stocking your kitchen for health is akin to laying a strong foundation for a house. It provides the essential building blocks that support a lifestyle centered around nutritious and flavorful meals. Picture this: a well-organized pantry brimming with wholesome staples, a refrigerator filled with fresh produce, and a spice cabinet offering a spectrum of flavors. Each component plays a pivotal role in transforming your culinary space into a haven of health and creativity.

Begin by focusing on the pantry, the heart of your kitchen's inventory. Whole grains such as brown rice, quinoa, oats, and whole wheat pasta should be staples. These grains serve as the backbone for a variety of meals, providing complex carbohydrates that deliver sustained energy. Legumes, including lentils, chickpeas, and black beans, are versatile proteins that enrich dishes with fiber and nutrients while offering a plant-based alternative to meat. Canned or dried, they have a long shelf life and can be easily incorporated into soups, stews, and salads.

Nuts and seeds are small but mighty, packed with healthy fats, protein, and essential vitamins. Almonds, walnuts, chia seeds, and flaxseeds are excellent choices, adding crunch and nutrition to both savory and sweet dishes. These can be sprinkled over yogurt, blended into smoothies, or used to garnish salads. Their versatility and nutrient density make them a pantry staple, perfect for snacking or enhancing meals.

Healthy oils are the cornerstone of cooking, with olive oil and coconut oil leading the pack. Olive oil, rich in monounsaturated fats, is ideal for salad dressings and low-heat cooking, while coconut oil's higher smoke point makes it suitable for baking and sautéing. Vinegars, such as apple cider and balsamic, bring acidity and balance to dishes, enhancing flavors without adding calories.

Herbs and spices are the soul of a flavorful and health-focused kitchen. Stocking a range of spices like cumin, turmeric, paprika, and cinnamon can transform bland meals into vibrant culinary experiences. Fresh herbs, such as basil, cilantro, and rosemary, add a burst of freshness and complexity to dishes. These seasonings not only elevate taste but also offer health benefits, with many boasting anti-inflammatory and antioxidant properties.

Transitioning to the refrigerator, fresh produce is key. A colorful array of fruits and vegetables ensures a wide intake of vitamins, minerals, and antioxidants. Leafy greens like spinach, kale, and arugula should be regulars in your fridge, offering a base for salads, smoothies, and side dishes. Cruciferous vegetables, such as broccoli, cauliflower, and Brussels sprouts, are nutrient powerhouses that support detoxification and overall health. Root vegetables, including carrots, beets, and sweet potatoes, provide natural sweetness and versatility, perfect for roasting or adding to soups.

Fruits, whether apples, berries, or citrus, offer natural sweetness and fiber. They make for a quick snack, a topping for breakfast bowls, or a refreshing dessert. Keeping a selection on hand encourages healthier snacking choices and adds color and flavor to meals.

Dairy or dairy alternatives are important for calcium and vitamin D. Greek yogurt, a high-protein option, can be used in both savory and sweet dishes, while plant-based milks like almond or oat milk provide lactose-free alternatives. Eggs are another refrigerator staple, versatile and packed with protein, suitable for breakfast, baking, or as a binder in recipes.

Proteins are essential for muscle repair and growth. Lean meats, such as chicken and turkey, offer low-fat options, while fish like salmon and tuna provide omega-3 fatty acids, which support heart health. For plant-based options, tofu and tempeh are excellent protein sources that can be marinated and cooked in various ways, adapting to countless recipes.

The freezer is an extension of the pantry and fridge, preserving ingredients for future use. Frozen fruits and vegetables retain their nutrients and can be used in smoothies, soups, or as side dishes. Freezing proteins like chicken breasts or fish fillets ensures a ready supply of ingredients, reducing the need for frequent grocery trips and minimizing food waste.

A well-stocked kitchen also considers convenience and accessibility. Organizing ingredients in a way that makes them easy to find and reach encourages home cooking and reduces reliance on takeout or processed meals. Clear labeling and categorization can help streamline the cooking process, making meal preparation more efficient and enjoyable.

Planning and periodic restocking are integral to maintaining a health-focused kitchen. Regularly assessing pantry and fridge contents allows for the timely replacement of staples and the introduction of new ingredients. Creating a weekly meal plan based on available ingredients can simplify grocery shopping and ensure a varied and balanced diet.

Ultimately, stocking your kitchen for health is about creating an environment that supports nutritious, delicious meals and encourages a sustainable, balanced lifestyle. By investing in quality ingredients and maintaining an organized space, you set the stage for culinary creativity and wellness, transforming daily cooking into a rewarding and healthful practice.

Chapter 2: Breakfast: Starting the Day Right

Energizing Morning Meals

A bright and nourishing start to the day can set the tone for everything that follows. Energizing morning meals are the cornerstone of a productive and vibrant day, providing the necessary fuel to power through tasks with vigor and clarity. Picture the morning sun streaming through your kitchen window, casting a warm glow over a table set with wholesome ingredients ready to be transformed into a breakfast feast.

The secret to a revitalizing breakfast lies in its ability to balance macronutrients—carbohydrates, proteins, and fats—while infusing the meal with a variety of flavors and textures. This harmony ensures sustained energy release, keeping hunger at bay until lunchtime and enhancing mental focus.

Begin with a base of complex carbohydrates, which provide a steady source of energy. Whole grains like oats, quinoa, and whole wheat bread are excellent choices. Oats, in particular, are a versatile staple. Consider a comforting bowl of oatmeal, simmered with almond milk, and topped with fresh berries and a sprinkle of nuts for added crunch. The soluble fiber in oats not only aids digestion but also helps maintain stable blood sugar levels, preventing the mid-morning energy slump.

Proteins are essential for muscle repair and satiety, making them a critical component of morning meals. Eggs are a classic breakfast option, celebrated for their versatility and nutrient density. A simple scramble with spinach and tomatoes, or a hearty omelet filled with peppers, mushrooms, and cheese, can be both satisfying and nourishing. For those seeking plant-based alternatives, consider a tofu scramble seasoned with turmeric and cumin, or a chia seed pudding topped with sliced bananas and a dollop of almond butter.

Healthy fats are another crucial element, aiding in the absorption of fat-soluble vitamins and providing a feeling of fullness. Avocado, with its creamy texture and mild flavor, is a popular choice. Spread it over toast, mash it into a smoothie, or slice it into a breakfast bowl. Nuts and seeds, such as almonds, walnuts, and flaxseeds, also contribute beneficial fats and can be effortlessly incorporated into a variety of dishes.

Incorporating fruits and vegetables into breakfast not only adds color and flavor but also boosts nutrient intake. Fresh berries, citrus fruits, and bananas are naturally sweet and rich in vitamins and antioxidants. Vegetables like tomatoes, bell peppers, and leafy greens can be tossed into omelets, blended into smoothies, or layered into breakfast wraps.

Hydration is a key aspect of an energizing morning routine. Starting the day with a glass of water or herbal tea can help rehydrate the body after a night's rest, enhancing cognitive function and digestion. For those who enjoy a morning coffee, consider adding a splash of plant-based milk or a sprinkle of cinnamon for an antioxidant boost.

Preparation is often the key to success, especially on busy mornings. Overnight oats provide a convenient option, allowing for a quick, grab-and-go breakfast. Simply combine oats, milk, seeds, and fruit in a jar, and let them soak overnight in the refrigerator. In the morning, a delicious and nutritious meal awaits, ready to be enjoyed at home or on the move.

Smoothies are another versatile and efficient breakfast choice, perfect for those with limited time. Blend a combination of leafy greens, frozen fruit, a scoop of protein powder, and a spoonful of nut butter for a nutrient-packed meal in a glass. The possibilities are endless, and the results are both refreshing and energizing.

For those who enjoy a more substantial breakfast, consider preparing a batch of whole-grain muffins or breakfast bars over the weekend. These can be stored in an airtight container and enjoyed throughout the week. Packed with oats, nuts, dried fruits, and a touch of honey, they offer a delightful balance of flavors and nutrients.

Cultural and personal preferences can shape breakfast choices and add diversity to the morning menu. Whether it's a traditional dish like a Spanish tortilla, an Indian masala omelet, or a Japanese miso soup with rice, incorporating elements from different cuisines can make breakfast an exciting culinary adventure.

Mindful eating practices can enhance the enjoyment and nourishment derived from breakfast. Taking a few moments to appreciate the colors, textures, and flavors of the meal can transform the act of eating into a meditative experience. This mindfulness promotes a more satisfying and fulfilling meal, setting a positive tone for the day.

Ultimately, energizing morning meals are about more than just food. They represent an opportunity to nourish the body, awaken the senses, and celebrate the start of a new day. By embracing this ritual with intention and creativity, each morning becomes a chance to cultivate health, happiness, and vitality.

Quick and Nutritious Breakfast Ideas

Mornings can often feel like a whirlwind, with the rush to get out the door leaving little time for a proper meal. Yet, breakfast remains one of the most crucial meals of the day, setting the tone for energy levels and concentration. The key is to discover breakfast ideas that are both quick and nutritious, providing the sustenance needed without sacrificing valuable time.

One of the simplest and most versatile options is the smoothie. With endless combinations of fruits, vegetables, proteins, and healthy fats, smoothies can be tailored to suit individual tastes and dietary needs. Begin with a liquid base—such as almond milk, coconut water, or plain yogurt—and add a handful of leafy greens like spinach or kale. These greens are mild in flavor while being rich in vitamins A, C, and K. Next, throw in a cup of frozen berries for natural sweetness and a dose of antioxidants. To boost the protein content, consider adding a scoop of protein powder or a spoonful of Greek yogurt. Finish with a tablespoon of chia seeds or flaxseeds, which provide omega-3 fatty acids and fiber, aiding digestion and keeping you full longer.

Another quick breakfast idea is overnight oats. This make-ahead meal is not only convenient but also allows for creativity with flavors and toppings. Combine rolled oats with your choice of milk or a dairy alternative in a jar. Add a sprinkle of cinnamon, a dollop of nut butter, and a handful of nuts or seeds. For sweetness, mix in a spoonful of honey or a few chopped dates. Seal the jar and let it sit in the refrigerator overnight. In the morning, you'll have a creamy and satisfying breakfast ready to go. Top with fresh fruit or a spoonful of yogurt for added texture and flavor.

For those who prefer a savory start, an egg muffin can be a lifesaver. These portable egg cups are simple to make in batches and can be stored in the fridge for several days. Start by whisking together eggs with a splash of milk, salt, and pepper. Pour the mixture into a muffin tin, filling each cup about halfway. Add your choice of vegetables, such as diced bell peppers, spinach, or mushrooms, and sprinkle with cheese or herbs. Bake in a preheated oven until the eggs are set and slightly golden. These muffins are perfect for reheating on busy mornings, offering a nutritious and protein-rich meal that's ready in minutes.

Avocado toast has gained popularity for good reason—it's quick, nutritious, and endlessly customizable. Begin with whole-grain or sourdough bread, toasted to your liking. Mash a ripe avocado with a pinch of salt, pepper, and a squeeze of lemon juice. Spread the mixture over the toast and add your favorite toppings. Sliced tomatoes, radishes, poached eggs, or a sprinkle of red pepper flakes can add extra flavor and nutrition. The healthy fats in avocado provide long-lasting energy and keep you feeling satisfied.

For a sweet option, consider yogurt parfaits. Layer Greek yogurt with granola and fresh fruit in a glass or bowl. Greek yogurt is an excellent source of protein and probiotics, supporting digestive health. Choose a granola that's low in sugar and high in fiber to maintain a balanced meal. Top with berries, sliced bananas, or a drizzle of honey for natural sweetness and additional vitamins.

For those who crave something warm and comforting, a quick breakfast porridge made from quinoa or amaranth can do the trick. Cook the grains with milk or a dairy-free alternative, adding a pinch of salt and a dash of vanilla extract. Once creamy, top with sliced almonds, dried fruit, or a spoonful of nut butter. These ancient grains are packed with protein and essential amino acids, making them a hearty and nutritious breakfast choice.

If you're in need of a grab-and-go option, homemade breakfast bars are ideal. Combine oats, nuts, seeds, and dried fruits in a large bowl. Add a binding agent like mashed banana or applesauce, along with a touch of honey or maple syrup for sweetness. Press the mixture into a baking dish and bake until set. Once cooled, cut into bars and wrap individually. These bars can be stored in an airtight container, providing a quick and nourishing breakfast for days when time is of the essence.

Even with the busiest of schedules, these quick and nutritious breakfast ideas demonstrate that it's possible to enjoy a wholesome start to the day. Each option can be adapted to suit personal preferences and dietary needs, ensuring a variety of flavors and nutrients. By incorporating these meals into your routine, you lay the foundation for a day filled with energy, focus, and well-being.

The Power of Smoothies and Bowls

Smoothies and bowls have emerged as powerhouses in the realm of healthy eating, beloved for their versatility, nutrient density, and vibrant appeal. Imagine starting your day with a refreshing smoothie, its colors as bright as the morning sun, or a beautifully composed bowl, each ingredient meticulously arranged like a painter's palette. These meals are not only visually captivating but also pack a punch of nutrition, making them ideal choices for individuals seeking a balanced and wholesome diet.

The allure of smoothies lies in their simplicity and endless customization. At their core, smoothies are a blend of fruits, vegetables, and liquids, yet their potential is limited only by imagination. Begin with a base liquid—such as almond milk, coconut water, or plain yogurt—to create a creamy consistency. From there, the possibilities expand exponentially. Imagine a tropical smoothie, where mango, pineapple, and a splash of orange juice transport you to a sun-drenched island with every sip. Or consider a green smoothie, where spinach, kale, and avocado blend harmoniously with a touch of apple for sweetness, delivering a powerful dose of vitamins and antioxidants.

Proteins and healthy fats can be seamlessly integrated into smoothies for sustained energy. A scoop of protein powder, a spoonful of Greek yogurt, or a handful of nuts can enhance the nutritional profile, making the smoothie more satiating. Flaxseeds, chia seeds, or a dollop of nut butter add healthy fats while contributing a delightful texture and flavor. These additions not only increase the nutritional value but also transform the smoothie into a complete meal capable of keeping hunger at bay for hours.

For those seeking a more substantial meal, smoothie bowls offer a thicker alternative, inviting creative toppings that add both texture and nutritional depth. A classic acai bowl, for instance, starts with a base of blended acai berries, bananas, and a splash of almond milk. The thick, luscious mixture is then adorned with an array of toppings: crunchy granola, sliced strawberries, coconut flakes, and a drizzle of honey. Each spoonful offers a delightful contrast of flavors and textures, making for a satisfying and indulgent breakfast or snack.

Smoothie bowls provide an excellent opportunity to incorporate a wider variety of ingredients. Consider a vibrant dragon fruit bowl, where the base of pink-hued dragon fruit is topped with kiwi slices, blueberries, and a sprinkle of hemp seeds. This nutrient-rich bowl not only pleases the eyes but also delivers a wealth of vitamins, minerals, and antioxidants essential for health and vitality.

The power of smoothies and bowls extends beyond their nutritional benefits. They are incredibly convenient, requiring minimal preparation and no cooking. For busy mornings or post-workout replenishment, a smoothie can be whipped up in minutes, providing a quick and nourishing meal on the go. Bowls, though slightly more involved, can be prepared in advance, with toppings added just before serving for maximum freshness and crunch.

These meals also offer a sustainable approach to eating, reducing food waste by utilizing ripe fruits and vegetables that might otherwise be discarded. Overripe bananas, wilting greens, and surplus berries can all find new life in a smoothie or bowl, transforming potential waste into culinary gold. This practice not only supports a more sustainable kitchen but also encourages creativity and resourcefulness in meal preparation.

In addition to their nutritional and practical benefits, smoothies and bowls foster mindfulness and intention in eating. Crafting a smoothie or bowl encourages a connection with the ingredients, a thoughtful selection of colors, flavors, and textures that reflect personal preferences and nutritional needs. This mindful approach extends to consumption, where savoring each sip or bite enhances the overall dining experience, promoting a deeper appreciation for the food and its role in nourishing the body.

For beginners venturing into the world of smoothies and bowls, start with familiar flavors and gradually experiment with new combinations. A classic banana and peanut butter smoothie can be a comforting introduction, while a berry and spinach bowl offers a gentle foray into incorporating greens. As confidence grows, explore more adventurous ingredients like matcha powder, spirulina, or goji berries, each bringing unique health benefits and flavors to the table.

Consider the seasonality of ingredients, as seasonal produce is often more flavorful and nutrient-dense. In summer, juicy peaches and berries make refreshing additions, while autumn calls for the warmth of cinnamon-spiced pumpkin and apple blends. This seasonal approach not only enhances flavor but also supports local agriculture and sustainability.

Incorporating smoothies and bowls into your routine can be a transformative step toward a healthier lifestyle. They offer a fun and flexible way to consume a variety of nutrients, cater to personal tastes, and adapt to any dietary preferences or restrictions. Whether enjoyed as a quick breakfast, a revitalizing snack, or a nourishing meal, these vibrant creations bring joy, health, and vitality to the dining experience. By embracing the power of smoothies and bowls, you open the door to a world of culinary exploration and well-being, one delicious blend at a time.

Incorporating Whole Grains

Whole grains are an integral component of a balanced diet, offering a myriad of health benefits while adding texture, flavor, and substance to meals. Imagine the nutty aroma of freshly cooked brown rice, the wholesome taste of whole wheat bread fresh from the oven, or the satisfying crunch of quinoa in a vibrant salad. Each grain tells a story of tradition and nourishment, deeply rooted in cultures across the globe.

Incorporating whole grains into your diet is a step towards improving overall health, as they are rich in fiber, essential nutrients, and antioxidants. Unlike refined grains, which have been stripped of their bran and germ, whole grains retain all parts of the grain kernel, preserving their nutritional integrity. This makes them a superior choice for those seeking a more nutrient-dense diet.

The journey to incorporating whole grains begins with understanding their variety and versatility. Familiar grains like brown rice, oats, and whole wheat are excellent starting points, but there are many others to explore, each offering unique flavors and culinary possibilities. Quinoa, an ancient grain revered by the Incas, is not only gluten-free but also a complete protein, containing all nine essential amino acids. Its slightly nutty flavor and delicate texture make it a versatile addition to salads, soups, and even breakfast bowls.

Barley, with its chewy texture and mild flavor, is another ancient grain worth exploring. It pairs beautifully with hearty vegetables and can be used in soups, stews, or as a base for grain salads. Farro, a staple in Italian cuisine, offers a delightful chew and a nutty flavor, perfect for risottos or as a side dish to roasted meats.

For those who enjoy baking, whole grains can transform homemade goods into healthier options. Whole wheat flour, spelt, and rye can replace refined flours in bread, muffins, and pancakes, adding depth of flavor and nutritional value. Experimenting with different grain flours can lead to the discovery of new textures and tastes, enriching the baking experience.

Incorporating whole grains into everyday meals can be both simple and rewarding. Start by substituting white rice with brown rice or quinoa, or replace white pasta with whole wheat or spelt varieties. These small changes can significantly increase fiber intake, promoting better digestion and prolonged satiety.

Breakfast is an ideal opportunity to introduce whole grains into your diet. Rolled oats or steel-cut oats make a hearty and nutritious base for porridge, topped with fresh fruits, nuts, and seeds. For a savory twist, consider adding sautéed greens and a poached egg. Whole grain cereals and granolas are also excellent choices, providing a quick and satisfying start to the day.

Salads can be elevated with the addition of whole grains, turning them into a complete meal. A Mediterranean-inspired salad with quinoa, cherry tomatoes, cucumbers, olives, and feta cheese offers a refreshing and nutrient-packed lunch. Barley or farro can be tossed with roasted vegetables and a simple vinaigrette for a wholesome side dish or main course.

Whole grains can also enhance soups and stews, adding texture and heartiness. A comforting vegetable and barley soup, simmered with herbs and spices, provides warmth and nourishment on a chilly day. Incorporating grains into these dishes not only boosts their nutritional profile but also stretches ingredients, making meals more economical.

For those new to whole grains, batch cooking is a practical approach. Preparing larger quantities of grains like quinoa, brown rice, or barley in advance ensures that they are readily available for meals throughout the week. Store them in airtight containers in the refrigerator, and they can be easily added to salads, stir-fries, or as a side dish.

Experimenting with international cuisines can also introduce you to new whole grains and preparation methods. Indian cuisine, for example, offers dishes like khichdi, a comforting combination of lentils and rice, often made with brown rice for added nutrition. Middle Eastern tabbouleh, traditionally made with bulgur wheat, is a refreshing salad perfect for warmer months.

Understanding the health benefits of whole grains can further motivate their inclusion in your diet. The high fiber content aids in regulating blood sugar levels and can help lower cholesterol, reducing the risk of heart disease. The abundance of vitamins and minerals, such as magnesium, iron, and B vitamins, supports overall health, including energy production and immune function.

Incorporating whole grains is not merely a dietary change but a lifestyle choice that fosters long-term wellness. By embracing the diversity and richness of whole grains, you open yourself to a world of flavors and culinary experiences that nourish both the body and the soul. This simple yet profound shift in eating habits can lead to a healthier, more balanced life, where each meal is an opportunity to savor the goodness of nature's bounty.

Protein-packed Breakfast Options

he morning sun peeks through the curtains, casting a gentle glow over your kitchen, where the promise of a protein-packed breakfast awaits. The importance of protein in the first meal of the day cannot be overstated, as it provides the essential building blocks for muscle repair, supports metabolic functions, and keeps hunger at bay. A well-balanced breakfast, rich in protein, can energize your morning and set a positive tone for the hours ahead.

Eggs are a classic breakfast staple and for good reason. They're a complete protein source, containing all nine essential amino acids. Their versatility allows for endless culinary possibilities. Imagine a fluffy omelet, filled with sautéed spinach, cherry tomatoes, and feta cheese. The vibrant colors and flavors create a sensory delight, while the protein content fuels your body. If you prefer a simpler preparation, a couple of poached or boiled eggs served with whole-grain toast and a side of avocado offers a satisfying and nutritious start.

For those seeking plant-based protein options, tofu scramble can be a delightful alternative. Crumble firm tofu into a pan with a dash of turmeric for color, and add in red bell peppers, onions, and spinach. Season with nutritional yeast for a cheesy flavor without the dairy. This dish not only delivers ample protein but also provides a hearty dose of vegetables, making it a balanced and energizing meal.

Greek yogurt is another protein powerhouse perfect for breakfast. Its creamy texture and tangy flavor make it a versatile base for a variety of dishes. Create a yogurt parfait with layers of Greek yogurt, mixed berries, and a sprinkle of granola or nuts. The combination of textures and flavors is not only pleasing to the palate but also ensures a meal rich in protein, fiber, and antioxidants. Alternatively, blend Greek yogurt into a smoothie with a banana, a scoop of protein powder, and a handful of spinach for a quick and nutrient-dense breakfast on the go.

For a heartier option, consider a breakfast burrito packed with protein-rich ingredients. Fill a whole-grain tortilla with scrambled eggs or tofu, black beans, diced tomatoes, and avocado. Add a dollop of salsa or hot sauce for a kick of flavor. This portable meal is perfect for busy mornings when you need a nutritious option that can be enjoyed on the move.

Quinoa, often celebrated as a superfood, makes an excellent addition to breakfast. Its high protein content and nutty flavor pair well with both sweet and savory ingredients. A warm quinoa breakfast bowl with almond milk, sliced almonds, and fresh berries offers a comforting and energizing start to the day. For a savory twist, cook quinoa with vegetable broth and mix in sautéed mushrooms, kale, and a poached egg.

Cottage cheese is another excellent source of protein that can be incorporated into breakfast in creative ways. Top a bowl of cottage cheese with sliced peaches and a sprinkle of cinnamon for a refreshing and protein-rich meal. For a savory option, pair cottage cheese with cherry tomatoes, sliced cucumbers, and a drizzle of olive oil. The possibilities are endless, and the nutritional benefits are significant.

For those who enjoy baking, protein-packed muffins can be a convenient breakfast option. Use whole-grain flour, eggs, Greek yogurt, and protein powder to create a batter rich in nutrients. Add in your favorite fruits or nuts for flavor and texture. These muffins can be made in batches and stored for quick breakfasts throughout the week.

Pancakes can also be transformed into a protein-rich breakfast with a few simple substitutions. Replace regular flour with almond flour or a protein pancake mix, and add eggs and cottage cheese to the batter. Serve with fresh berries and a dollop of Greek yogurt for a delicious and nutritious twist on a breakfast classic.

For a more traditional breakfast, consider a serving of smoked salmon on whole-grain toast with cream cheese, capers, and red onion. The combination of flavors and textures is both satisfying and rich in protein, omega-3 fatty acids, and essential nutrients.

Incorporating protein into breakfast doesn't have to be complicated or time-consuming. With a little planning and creativity, you can enjoy a variety of delicious and nutritious meals that keep you energized and satisfied throughout the morning. By prioritizing protein, you support your body's needs and set the stage for a day filled with vitality and well-being. Whether you prefer eggs, tofu, yogurt, or quinoa, the options are plentiful, catering to diverse tastes and dietary preferences. Embrace the power of protein and transform your breakfast into a foundation for health and happiness.

Chapter 3: Lunches that Satisfy and Nourish

Crafting Balanced Midday Meals

A balanced midday meal is the linchpin of a productive day, offering the necessary nourishment to keep you energized and focused through the afternoon. Imagine sitting down to a meal that not only satisfies your hunger but also invigorates your senses with vibrant colors, rich flavors, and diverse textures. Crafting such meals requires a thoughtful approach, emphasizing the importance of variety and balance.

At the heart of a balanced midday meal is the harmonious combination of macronutrients: carbohydrates, proteins, and fats. Each plays a vital role in maintaining energy levels, supporting bodily functions, and promoting satiety, preventing the post-lunch energy slump that often leads to afternoon cravings.

Carbohydrates, particularly complex ones, serve as the primary energy source. Whole grains, legumes, and starchy vegetables like sweet potatoes provide slow-releasing energy, helping to maintain stable blood sugar levels. Consider a quinoa salad, where fluffy grains mingle with roasted vegetables and a splash of lemon vinaigrette. The textures and flavors create an engaging dining experience, while the nutrients provide sustained energy.

Proteins are essential for muscle repair and overall health. Lean meats, fish, eggs, and plant-based options like beans and lentils can be seamlessly integrated into midday meals. A grilled chicken breast, seasoned with herbs and olive oil, pairs beautifully with a medley of roasted root vegetables. Alternatively, a chickpea and spinach stew, simmered with tomatoes and spices, offers a hearty vegetarian option, rich in flavor and protein.

Healthy fats are crucial for brain function and the absorption of fat-soluble vitamins. Avocados, nuts, seeds, and olive oil are excellent sources that can enhance the taste and nutritional profile of meals. Picture a vibrant salad topped with creamy avocado slices, a handful of toasted walnuts, and a drizzle of balsamic glaze. Each bite delivers a satisfying crunch and a burst of flavor, while nourishing the body.

Incorporating a variety of vegetables into midday meals not only adds color and appeal but also boosts the intake of vitamins, minerals, and fiber. Leafy greens, bell peppers, tomatoes, and cruciferous vegetables like broccoli and cauliflower contribute a wealth of nutrients. A roasted vegetable and farro bowl, adorned with a sprinkle of feta cheese and fresh herbs, can be both a feast for the eyes and a nourishing meal.

Mindful portion control plays a significant role in crafting balanced meals. Paying attention to hunger cues and serving appropriate portions helps avoid overeating and ensures that meals are both satisfying and energizing. Start with a plate divided into sections: one-half filled with vegetables, one-quarter with protein, and one-quarter with carbohydrates. This visual guide can assist in creating balanced meals without the need for meticulous measuring.

Preparation is key to successful midday meals, especially during the workweek. Preparing larger batches of grains, proteins, and roasted vegetables in advance can save time and make assembling meals more efficient. Store these components in airtight containers, ready to be mixed and matched for a variety of meals throughout the week.

International cuisines offer a treasure trove of inspiration for balanced midday meals. A Mediterranean-inspired platter with hummus, olives, roasted red peppers, and whole-grain pita invites exploration of flavors and textures. Similarly, a Mexican-style bowl with black beans, brown rice, grilled vegetables, and a sprinkle of cheese provides a satisfying and balanced meal.

Hydration is an often-overlooked aspect of midday nourishment. Ensuring adequate fluid intake is essential for maintaining energy levels and cognitive function. Water, herbal teas, or infusions with slices of citrus and fresh herbs can complement meals and contribute to overall hydration.

For those who dine away from home, packing a balanced lunch can be both economical and health-conscious. A sturdy container with compartments can keep different elements of the meal separate and fresh. Sandwiches on whole-grain bread with lean protein and plenty of vegetables, grain-based salads with beans and a zesty dressing, or a wrap filled with colorful veggies and a protein source are all portable and satisfying options.

Crafting balanced midday meals is not only about meeting nutritional needs but also celebrating the joy of eating. Taking time to savor each bite, appreciating the flavors and textures, can transform a meal from a mere necessity into a pleasurable experience. This mindful approach to eating fosters a deeper connection with food and encourages healthier choices.

Ultimately, the art of crafting balanced midday meals lies in embracing variety and creativity. By incorporating a diverse array of ingredients and flavors, you not only nourish your body but also cultivate a sense of culinary adventure. Each meal becomes an opportunity to explore, enjoy, and sustain well-being, paving the way for a productive and fulfilling day.

Creative Salad Inspirations

Salads have long evolved from their humble beginnings as simple side dishes to vibrant culinary masterpieces bursting with colors, textures, and flavors. Imagine a canvas where each ingredient is a stroke of artistry, creating a harmonious blend that delights both the eye and the palate. Crafting a salad is an opportunity to unleash your creativity, experimenting with different combinations while ensuring a balance of nutrients in every bite.

A great salad begins with a base, and the options are endless. Traditional greens like romaine, spinach, and arugula provide a fresh and crisp foundation. Each leaf brings its own character: the mild sweetness of spinach, the peppery bite of arugula, the crunchy texture of romaine. For a more adventurous twist, consider using kale, Swiss chard, or even cabbage, finely shredded to add a hearty and robust texture.

The heart of salad creativity lies in the toppings. Vegetables, fruits, proteins, grains, nuts, and seeds all play their part in creating a unique and nutritious dish. Consider the vibrant hues of bell peppers, the juicy sweetness of cherry tomatoes, or the earthy flavor of roasted beets. Each ingredient adds a different dimension, enhancing both the visual appeal and the nutritional value.

Fruits introduce an unexpected yet delightful sweetness. Slices of ripe mango, juicy pomegranate seeds, or tart apple slices can transform the flavor profile of a salad, creating an intriguing balance with savory elements. Meanwhile, proteins such as grilled chicken, tofu, or chickpeas provide substance and satiety, turning a simple salad into a fulfilling meal.

Grains add heartiness and texture, making salads more substantial. Quinoa, farro, or barley can serve as a wonderful base or a nourishing topping. These grains not only provide a chewy texture but also introduce a nutty flavor and a wealth of nutrients. A quinoa salad with roasted vegetables, chickpeas, and a zesty lemon-tahini dressing can be both refreshing and satisfying.

Nuts and seeds bring a satisfying crunch and a dose of healthy fats. Toasted almonds, sunflower seeds, or pumpkin seeds can elevate a salad with their rich flavors and textures. Consider a spinach salad topped with goat cheese, strawberries, and a sprinkle of slivered almonds for a delightful symphony of flavors.

Dressings are the final flourish, the element that ties all the ingredients together. A simple vinaigrette made with olive oil, balsamic vinegar, and Dijon mustard is a classic choice. For a creamier option, a Greek yogurt-based dressing with herbs and lemon can add a refreshing tang. The key is to balance the acidity and sweetness, enhancing the natural flavors of the salad without overpowering them.

Creating a salad is not only about the individual components but also about how they interact. The textures of crunchy, crisp, and creamy, the flavors of sweet, savory, and tangy—all these elements come together to form a cohesive and delightful dish. A well-crafted salad is a testament to the harmonious blend of ingredients, where each component complements the other.

For those new to the art of salad making, start with familiar combinations and gradually introduce new ingredients. A classic Caesar salad with romaine, croutons, Parmesan cheese, and a tangy dressing can be a comforting starting point. As confidence grows, experiment with more exotic ingredients like roasted figs, grilled peaches, or even edible flowers for a touch of elegance.

The beauty of salads lies in their adaptability to different seasons. In the summer, a refreshing watermelon and feta salad with mint can provide a cooling respite from the heat. In the fall, a roasted butternut squash salad with kale and cranberries offers warmth and richness, celebrating the flavors of the harvest.

Salads can also be a reflection of global cuisines, each culture offering its own unique twist. A classic Greek salad with tomatoes, cucumbers, olives, and feta cheese transports you to the sun-drenched Mediterranean. A Thai-inspired salad with green papaya, peanuts, and a spicy lime dressing offers a burst of exotic flavors.

Beyond the nutritional benefits, salads promote mindfulness and intention in eating. The process of selecting fresh ingredients, preparing them with care, and arranging them artfully on a plate encourages a deeper appreciation for food. This mindful approach extends to consumption, where each bite is savored, enhancing the overall dining experience.

Incorporating salads into your routine can be a transformative step toward a healthier lifestyle. They offer an enjoyable and flexible way to consume a variety of nutrients, catering to personal tastes and dietary preferences. Whether enjoyed as a light starter, a side dish, or a main course, salads bring joy, health, and vibrancy to the dining experience. By embracing the creative potential of salads, you open the door to a world of culinary exploration and well-being, one delicious bowl at a time.

Hearty Soups and Stews

The comforting allure of a steaming bowl of soup or stew is unparalleled, especially on a chilly day when warmth and nourishment are most needed. These hearty dishes, steeped in tradition and culture, offer a sense of home and hospitality with every spoonful. Imagine the rich aroma wafting through the kitchen, a medley of spices and herbs mingling with simmering vegetables and tender meats, creating a symphony of flavors that invites you to savor each bite.

Soups and stews are not just about sustenance; they are a celebration of simplicity and depth. The process of slow cooking allows flavors to meld and intensify, transforming humble ingredients into a dish of complexity and delight. The beauty of these meals lies in their versatility, using whatever is fresh or available to create something uniquely satisfying.

Start with the foundation—a flavorful broth or stock. Whether it's a robust beef stock, a delicate chicken broth, or a rich vegetable base, the quality of the stock sets the tone for the entire dish. Homemade stocks, simmered with bones, herbs, and aromatics, provide a depth of flavor that store-bought versions often lack. However, for those pressed for time, quality store-bought options can also serve as a reliable base.

Vegetables play a starring role in soups and stews, contributing both flavor and nutrition. Carrots, celery, and onions, often referred to as the "holy trinity" in cooking, provide a classic aromatic base. Root vegetables like potatoes, parsnips, and sweet potatoes add heartiness and texture. Leafy greens, such as kale and spinach, can be stirred in towards the end of cooking to preserve their vibrant color and nutritional value.

Proteins, whether animal or plant-based, offer substance and satisfaction. Tender chunks of beef, succulent pieces of chicken, or delicate fish can enhance the richness of a stew. For a vegetarian or vegan option, lentils, beans, and tofu provide protein while absorbing the flavors of the broth. Consider a classic beef stew, where cubes of beef are browned and slowly cooked with red wine, mushrooms, and herbs, creating a dish of comforting depth. Alternatively, a Moroccan chickpea stew, infused with cumin, coriander, and cinnamon, offers a fragrant and hearty vegetarian option.

Herbs and spices are the soul of any good soup or stew, infusing the dish with character and warmth. Bay leaves, thyme, and rosemary add a touch of earthiness, while spices like cumin, paprika, and chili flakes introduce warmth and complexity. A dash of freshly ground pepper or a sprinkle of sea salt can elevate the flavors, bringing balance and harmony to the dish.

The method of preparation is just as important as the ingredients themselves. Browning meats and vegetables before adding them to the pot creates a rich, caramelized flavor that enhances the overall depth of the stew. Deglazing the pan with wine or broth can lift those flavorful bits from the bottom of the pan, incorporating them into the stock. Allowing the soup or stew to simmer gently, occasionally stirring and tasting, ensures that the flavors develop fully and that the ingredients are cooked to perfection.

For those new to the art of making soups and stews, start with a classic recipe and gradually experiment with new ingredients and techniques. A traditional chicken noodle soup, with its delicate broth and tender pieces of chicken, is both comforting and simple to prepare. Once comfortable, try adding different herbs or vegetables to create new flavor profiles.

Seasonal ingredients can guide your choice of soups and stews. In winter, a hearty minestrone with beans, pasta, and winter vegetables offers warmth and nutrition. In summer, a chilled gazpacho, made with ripe tomatoes, cucumbers, and peppers, provides a refreshing and light alternative.

Beyond their comforting flavors, soups and stews offer practical benefits. They are perfect for batch cooking, allowing for leftovers that can be enjoyed throughout the week or frozen for later convenience. This makes them an economical choice, reducing food waste and maximizing the use of available ingredients.

Presentation can elevate a simple bowl of soup or stew into an inviting meal. A sprinkle of fresh herbs, a drizzle of cream, or a slice of crusty bread on the side can transform the dish into a feast for the senses. The joy of serving a beautifully crafted bowl of soup or stew lies not only in the flavors but in the warmth and hospitality it conveys.

The art of making hearty soups and stews is a journey of exploration and satisfaction. By experimenting with different ingredients, techniques, and flavors, you can create dishes that are not only nourishing but also deeply fulfilling. Whether shared with family and friends or savored alone, a well-prepared soup or stew is a testament to the joys of cooking and the comforting power of food. Embrace the process, savor the results, and let each bowl tell its own delicious story.

Wholesome Sandwich and Wrap Options

The humble sandwich, a staple in many households, offers endless possibilities for creativity and nourishment. From the bustling streets of New York with its towering deli sandwiches to the quaint cafes of Paris serving delicate baguettes, sandwiches have become a universal symbol of convenience and versatility. The beauty of a sandwich lies in its ability to transform simple ingredients into a satisfying and portable meal, perfect for any time of day.

At the core of an exceptional sandwich is the bread. Whether you opt for whole grain, sourdough, rye, or a gluten-free alternative, the choice of bread sets the foundation for the flavors and textures that follow. Imagine the crisp crust of a freshly baked baguette or the robust flavor of a dark rye, each offering a unique canvas for your culinary creations.

Proteins are often the star of the sandwich, providing both substance and flavor. For those who enjoy meat, consider options such as roasted turkey, grilled chicken, or sliced roast beef. Each brings its own character, from the smoky aroma of grilled meats to the delicate savoriness of slow-roasted deli cuts. Plant-based eaters can explore the richness of marinated tofu, the heartiness of roasted chickpeas, or the creaminess of smashed avocado.

Cheese can add a layer of richness and complexity to sandwiches. From the sharp tang of aged cheddar to the creamy decadence of brie, cheese enhances both flavor and texture. However, for a lighter option, consider using a smear of hummus, a dollop of tzatziki, or a spread of tangy mustard to add moisture and zest.

Vegetables play a crucial role in sandwiches, offering freshness, crunch, and a burst of color. Leafy greens like lettuce, arugula, or spinach add a vibrant layer, while slices of tomato, cucumber, and bell pepper contribute juiciness and brightness. For a touch of sweetness, consider adding thin slices of apple or pear, which pair beautifully with both savory and creamy elements.

Condiments and spreads are the finishing touches that bring a sandwich to life. A swipe of Dijon mustard, a spoonful of pesto, or a layer of chipotle mayo can infuse a sandwich with distinctive flavors. These elements bind the ingredients together, creating a harmonious blend that delights the palate with each bite.

Wraps offer an alternative to traditional sandwiches, using flatbreads or tortillas to encase the ingredients. The flexibility of a wrap allows for creative fillings, from the classic combination of turkey and avocado to more adventurous pairings like falafel with pickled vegetables and tahini. The key to a successful wrap is in the balance of textures and flavors, ensuring that each ingredient complements the others without overwhelming the whole.

Preparation techniques can significantly enhance the enjoyment of sandwiches and wraps. Toasting the bread or wrap can bring out the natural flavors and add a delightful crunch. Grilling a sandwich, like a classic panini, melts the cheese to perfection while creating a satisfying contrast between the crispy exterior and the warm, gooey interior. For wraps, a quick sear on a hot skillet can seal the edges and add a toasty flavor.

For beginners eager to experiment, start with a classic and build on it. A traditional club sandwich with turkey, bacon, lettuce, and tomato is a reliable favorite. From there, add personal touches—perhaps a sprinkle of fresh herbs, a slice of avocado, or a drizzle of balsamic reduction—to make it uniquely yours.

Seasonal ingredients can also inspire sandwich and wrap options. In the summer, a caprese sandwich with fresh mozzarella, ripe tomatoes, basil, and a balsamic glaze offers a taste of the season's bounty. In the fall, a roast vegetable and goat cheese wrap, featuring squash and beets, provides warmth and richness.

Beyond their culinary appeal, sandwiches and wraps are practical. They can be prepared quickly, making them ideal for busy days, and are easily portable, perfect for lunches, picnics, or road trips. With a little planning, they can also be an economical choice, using leftovers or pantry staples to create a delicious meal.

Presentation can elevate a simple sandwich or wrap into a gourmet experience. Consider cutting sandwiches diagonally for visual appeal or wrapping them in parchment paper for a rustic touch. A side of pickles, a handful of mixed greens, or a small bowl of soup can complete the meal, adding variety and balance.

The art of crafting wholesome sandwiches and wraps is a journey of discovery and delight. By exploring different ingredients, textures, and flavors, you can create meals that are not only nourishing but also a joy to eat. Whether enjoyed alone or shared with friends and family, these creations celebrate the simplicity and satisfaction of good food. Embrace the endless possibilities, savor each creation, and let your culinary imagination run wild with every sandwich and wrap you make.

Meal Prepping for Busy Days

The hustle and bustle of daily life often leave little room for thoughtful meal preparation, yet the importance of nourishing meals cannot be overstated. Meal prepping emerges as a beacon of efficiency, allowing individuals to maintain a healthy diet despite their hectic schedules. Picture a Sunday afternoon where the kitchen becomes a hub of activity, with fresh ingredients spread across the counter, ready to be transformed into a week's worth of meals. The satisfaction of having a well-stocked fridge, filled with ready-to-eat or easy-to-assemble meals, can alleviate the stress of daily meal planning and ensure that nutritious options are always within reach.

The art of meal prepping begins with a plan. Consider your weekly schedule, identifying days when time is particularly limited and meals need to be quick and convenient. With this in mind, build a menu that caters to your tastes, dietary needs, and the amount of time you realistically have to prepare and consume each meal. A balanced approach, incorporating a variety of proteins, grains, vegetables, and healthy fats, ensures that meals remain interesting and nutritious.

Once a menu is established, create a comprehensive shopping list. This step helps streamline the grocery shopping experience, reducing the likelihood of impulse purchases and ensuring that all necessary ingredients are on hand. Fresh produce, lean proteins, whole grains, and pantry staples form the backbone of meal prep, providing a versatile foundation for a multitude of dishes.

The preparation itself can be approached in several ways, depending on personal preference and available time. Batch cooking is a popular method, involving the preparation of large quantities of staple components like grains, proteins, and roasted vegetables. Quinoa, brown rice, or whole-grain pasta can be cooked in advance, while chicken breasts, tofu, or legumes can be seasoned and roasted or grilled. These elements can then be mixed and matched throughout the week to create a variety of meals.

Another approach involves preparing complete meals that can be stored in individual containers, ready to be reheated and enjoyed. Casseroles, stir-fries, and hearty salads are excellent candidates for this method. Imagine opening the fridge to find a colorful array of meals, each one carefully portioned and bursting with flavor, waiting to be savored. The convenience of having meals ready to go can be a game-changer, particularly on days when time is of the essence.

When it comes to storing prepped meals, organization is key. Invest in a set of high-quality, airtight containers that are microwave and dishwasher safe. Clear containers allow you to easily see the contents, reducing the likelihood of forgotten meals languishing in the back of the fridge. Label containers with the date and contents to keep track of freshness and ensure that meals are consumed in a timely manner.

A vital aspect of successful meal prepping is variety. To avoid monotony, incorporate a range of flavors, textures, and cuisines into your menu. For example, a Mediterranean-inspired bowl with quinoa, grilled chicken, olives, and tzatziki can be followed by a Thai-inspired stir-fry with tofu, vegetables, and a spicy peanut sauce. Experiment with different spices and herbs to keep meals exciting and flavorful.

Meal prepping is not limited to lunches and dinners. Breakfasts and snacks can also benefit from a little advance planning. Overnight oats, smoothie packs, and homemade energy bars can be prepared in batches, ensuring that healthy options are readily available to start the day on the right foot or to provide a midday energy boost.

For beginners, the prospect of meal prepping can seem daunting, but it need not be. Start small, perhaps by preparing just a few meals or snacks each week, gradually increasing as confidence and experience grow. The key is to find a system that works for you, adapting and refining your approach as needed.

The benefits of meal prepping extend beyond mere convenience. By taking control of your meals, you gain greater insight into your eating habits, allowing for more mindful and intentional choices. This practice can lead to healthier eating patterns, reduce reliance on takeout or processed foods, and ultimately contribute to overall well-being.

Moreover, meal prepping can be a rewarding and enjoyable process. The act of preparing meals with care and intention fosters a deeper appreciation for the food you consume. It also provides an opportunity to involve family or friends, turning what might otherwise be a solitary task into a shared experience.

Incorporating meal prepping into your routine can transform the way you approach eating, offering a practical solution to the challenges of a busy lifestyle. With a little planning, creativity, and dedication, you can ensure that nutritious and delicious meals are always within easy reach, supporting your health and well-being every day. Embrace the efficiency and freedom that meal prepping provides, and enjoy the peace of mind that comes with knowing you are nourishing your body with care and intention.

Chapter 4: Dinner Delights for Health and Flavor

Exploring Global Cuisines

The world of culinary arts is a vast tapestry of flavors, traditions, and innovations, each thread representing the rich heritage of a different culture. Exploring global cuisines is akin to embarking on a journey around the world, where each dish tells a story of history, geography, and the human spirit's ingenuity. Imagine the sizzle of a wok in a bustling Asian market, the aromatic spices perfuming the air, or the warmth of a communal table in a Mediterranean village, laden with rustic breads and vibrant salads. Each experience opens a window into a different way of life, offering a glimpse into the heart of a culture.

Italian cuisine, celebrated for its emphasis on fresh ingredients and simplicity, is a testament to the adage that less is often more. A classic Margherita pizza, with its thin, crispy crust, fresh tomato sauce, mozzarella, and basil, embodies the spirit of Naples. The pasta dishes, whether it's a creamy carbonara or a hearty Bolognese, showcase the Italians' love affair with this versatile staple. The key to Italian cooking lies in using the freshest ingredients available, allowing their natural flavors to shine.

In contrast, Indian cuisine is a vibrant explosion of colors, aromas, and textures. Known for its extensive use of spices, Indian cooking offers a sensory experience like no other. The complexity of a well-made curry, with its layers of spices building upon one another, is a testament to the skill and intuition of the cook. Dishes like biryani, a fragrant rice dish with meat or vegetables, and masala dosa, a crispy crepe filled with spiced potatoes, illustrate the diversity within Indian cuisine, reflecting the many regions and cultures within the country.

Mexican cuisine, with its bold flavors and rich traditions, offers a feast for the senses. The use of chilies, corn, and beans, staples that date back to ancient civilizations, forms the backbone of many dishes. Envision a plate of tacos al pastor, with marinated pork, pineapple, and fresh cilantro, or a bowl of pozole, a hearty soup made with hominy and pork, garnished with radishes and lime. The vibrant flavors and communal nature of Mexican meals make them both inviting and comforting.

The delicate balance of flavors in Japanese cuisine reflects a deep respect for harmony and seasonality. Sushi, perhaps the most recognized Japanese dish, is a perfect example of this philosophy. The artful presentation, the freshness of the fish, and the subtle seasoning of the rice all contribute to a harmonious whole. Beyond sushi, dishes like ramen, with its rich broth and variety of toppings, and tempura, lightly battered and fried seafood or vegetables, showcase the precision and attention to detail inherent in Japanese cooking.

French cuisine, with its emphasis on technique and tradition, is often considered the pinnacle of culinary arts. The mastery of sauces, the art of pastry, and the elegance of presentation are hallmarks of French cooking. A classic coq au vin, with its tender chicken braised in red wine, or a buttery croissant, flaky and golden, highlight the sophistication and depth of flavor that are the hallmarks of this cuisine. French dining is as much about the experience as it is about the food, with an emphasis on savoring each course and enjoying the company of others.

Middle Eastern cuisine, rich with aromatic spices and hearty staples, is a celebration of hospitality and generosity. Dishes like hummus, a creamy blend of chickpeas and tahini, and falafel, crispy and flavorful chickpea fritters, are both satisfying and nutritious. The mezze platter, with its array of small dishes like tabbouleh, baba ghanoush, and kibbeh, encourages sharing and conversation, embodying the communal spirit of Middle Eastern dining.

Exploring these global cuisines requires an open mind and a willingness to experiment with unfamiliar ingredients and techniques. Start by selecting a cuisine that intrigues you, researching its traditional dishes, and gathering the necessary ingredients. Many ethnic markets offer a treasure trove of spices, produce, and specialty items that are essential for authentic preparation. Cooking from a different culture not only broadens your palate but also deepens your appreciation for the diversity and creativity of the world's culinary traditions.

For beginners, it may be helpful to start with a specific dish or ingredient that piques your interest. Perhaps it's the allure of a fragrant Thai green curry, with its blend of coconut milk, green chilies, and fresh herbs, or the simplicity of a Spanish paella, with its saffron-infused rice and seafood. By focusing on one dish at a time, you can gradually build your skills and confidence, eventually expanding to more complex recipes and techniques.

Engaging with global cuisines is not only about cooking but also about understanding the cultural context in which these foods are enjoyed. Each dish is a reflection of the land, climate, and people who created it, offering insights into their way of life. Whether it's the tradition of Italian families gathering for Sunday pasta, the Japanese tea ceremony's ritualistic precision, or the vibrant celebrations of Mexican fiestas, food is a unifying force that brings people together.

Incorporating elements of global cuisines into your everyday cooking can be both exciting and rewarding. By learning from different culinary traditions, you can infuse new flavors and techniques into your own cooking repertoire, creating dishes that are uniquely yours. This exploration not only expands your culinary horizons but also fosters a greater appreciation for the richness and diversity of the world we live in.

Ultimately, the journey of exploring global cuisines is a celebration of the human spirit's creativity and adaptability. Each dish tells a story, each flavor a note in the symphony of life. By embracing the world's culinary diversity, you open yourself to a world of new experiences, connections, and joys, one delicious bite at a time.

Plant-based Dinner Ideas

The rise of plant-based eating is not merely a trend but a conscious shift towards a more sustainable and health-conscious way of living. With an abundance of fresh produce, grains, legumes, and nuts, the world of plant-based cooking offers endless possibilities for creating delicious and satisfying meals. Imagine a dinner table brimming with vibrant colors, aromatic herbs, and diverse textures—each dish a testament to the creativity and ingenuity that plant-based cuisine inspires.

One of the simplest and most versatile plant-based dinner ideas is the grain bowl. Start with a base of nutrient-rich grains such as quinoa, farro, or brown rice. These grains provide a hearty foundation, offering both substance and nutritional benefits. Top the grains with a medley of seasonal vegetables, roasted to perfection. The caramelization process brings out the natural sweetness of vegetables like carrots, bell peppers, and Brussels sprouts. Add a protein component with chickpeas, lentils, or tofu, seasoned with herbs and spices to enhance their flavor profile. Finish with a drizzle of tahini dressing or a squeeze of lemon juice for a fresh, tangy finish.

Stir-fries are another excellent option for plant-based dinners, allowing for quick preparation and endless customization. Begin with a selection of your favorite vegetables—broccoli, snap peas, and mushrooms work particularly well. Sauté them in a hot pan with a splash of sesame oil, adding garlic and ginger for a fragrant foundation. Incorporate tofu or tempeh for protein, letting them absorb the flavors of the sauce. For the sauce, a mixture of soy sauce, rice vinegar, and a hint of maple syrup can create a balance of savory, tangy, and sweet notes. Serve the stir-fry over a bed of steamed rice or noodles for a complete meal that's both satisfying and nourishing.

For those seeking comfort food, a plant-based shepherd's pie can be a hearty and warming option. Replace the traditional meat filling with a mixture of lentils, mushrooms, and vegetables such as carrots and peas. This combination creates a rich and savory base, full of umami flavors. Top with creamy mashed potatoes, made with plant-based milk and a touch of olive oil for smoothness. Bake the pie until the top is golden brown and the filling is bubbling, resulting in a dish that's as comforting as it is wholesome.

Another delightful plant-based dinner idea is a vegetable curry, a dish that celebrates the bold flavors of spices. Start by sautéing onions, garlic, and ginger in coconut oil until fragrant. Add a blend of spices such as cumin, coriander, and turmeric, allowing them to release their aromas. Introduce a variety of vegetables like sweet potatoes, cauliflower, and spinach, letting them simmer in coconut milk until tender. The result is a creamy, aromatic curry that pairs beautifully with basmati rice or naan bread.

For a lighter option, consider preparing a refreshing plant-based salad, one that goes beyond the typical leafy greens. Use a base of kale or spinach, massaged with a bit of olive oil to soften the leaves. Add roasted beets, slices of avocado, and segments of citrus fruits like oranges or grapefruits. Sprinkle with toasted nuts or seeds for crunch, and dress with a vinaigrette made from balsamic vinegar and mustard. The combination of flavors and textures creates a salad that's both vibrant and satisfying.

Tacos offer a fun and interactive dinner option, perfect for showcasing the versatility of plant-based ingredients. Use corn or flour tortillas as a base and fill them with a variety of components. Roasted vegetables, black beans, and fresh salsa can make for a delicious filling. Add a dollop of guacamole or cashew cream for creaminess, and garnish with cilantro and lime for freshness. The beauty of tacos lies in their adaptability; each person can customize their own, making it a perfect dish for gatherings.

Incorporating plant-based proteins into your dinners is a key aspect of maintaining a balanced diet. Beans, lentils, and tofu are excellent sources of protein, each offering unique textures and flavors. Experiment with different cooking methods, such as roasting, grilling, or marinating, to enhance these ingredients' natural qualities. For instance, marinated tofu skewers, grilled to perfection, can be served with a side of quinoa and steamed vegetables for a complete meal.

Soups and stews are also comforting plant-based options, ideal for cooler evenings. A classic minestrone, packed with seasonal vegetables and beans, is both nourishing and hearty. For a creamier option, consider a butternut squash soup, blended until smooth and seasoned with nutmeg and cinnamon for warmth. These dishes can be prepared in advance, allowing the flavors to develop over time, making them even more delicious when served.

For those new to plant-based cooking, it's important to embrace experimentation and creativity. Start by incorporating more plant-based meals into your weekly routine, gradually exploring new ingredients and recipes. The key is to focus on whole, unprocessed foods, highlighting their natural flavors and textures. With time, you'll discover a world of possibilities, from vibrant salads to comforting stews, each meal a celebration of the abundance of plant-based ingredients.

Plant-based dinners offer not only health benefits but also a connection to nature and the earth's bounty. By embracing this way of eating, you contribute to a more sustainable and compassionate world, where every meal is a step towards a brighter future. Enjoy the journey of discovering plant-based cuisine, and relish the joy and fulfillment it brings to your table.

Lean Proteins and Healthy Fats

The journey to a balanced diet often leads to the discovery of two vital components: lean proteins and healthy fats. These nutrients are crucial for maintaining energy levels, supporting muscle growth, and promoting overall health. While the word "protein" might conjure images of dense steaks or hearty burgers, there's a wide array of lean options that can provide the necessary nutrients without the excess saturated fat. Similarly, healthy fats, often misunderstood, are essential for brain function, hormone production, and cellular health. Together, they form a powerful duo that supports a vibrant and active lifestyle.

Lean proteins are an excellent source of amino acids, the building blocks of the body. They help repair tissues, produce enzymes and hormones, and support immune function. For those looking to incorporate more lean proteins into their diet, the options are diverse and flavorful. Skinless poultry, such as chicken or turkey, is a versatile choice that can be grilled, baked, or sautéed. These meats absorb marinades and spices well, allowing for creativity in seasoning and preparation. Imagine a rosemary and lemon grilled chicken breast, juicy and aromatic, served with a side of steamed vegetables—a meal that is both satisfying and light.

Fish, particularly fatty fish like salmon, trout, and mackerel, offers a double benefit of being both a lean protein and a source of healthy omega-3 fatty acids. These fats are known for their role in reducing inflammation and supporting heart health. A fillet of broiled salmon, with its rich, buttery texture, can be complemented by a squeeze of fresh lemon and a sprinkle of dill. Not only is it delicious, but it also provides essential nutrients that nourish the body from the inside out.

For those who prefer plant-based options, legumes such as beans, lentils, and chickpeas are excellent sources of lean protein. They are also rich in fiber, which aids in digestion and helps maintain a feeling of fullness. A hearty lentil soup, simmered with vegetables and spices, or a chickpea salad tossed with fresh herbs and a light vinaigrette, can make for a fulfilling meal. Tofu and tempeh are other versatile plant-based proteins that can be marinated and cooked in various ways to suit different cuisines and tastes.

Eggs, often dubbed nature's perfect food, are a compact source of high-quality protein. They are rich in vitamins and minerals, including B vitamins and choline, important for brain health. Whether scrambled, poached, or boiled, eggs can be a quick and nutritious meal or snack. Consider a vegetable omelet for breakfast, packed with spinach, tomatoes, and onions, providing a balanced start to the day.

Healthy fats, on the other hand, are crucial for maintaining cellular integrity and supporting neurological function. While it might seem counterintuitive, consuming the right types of fats can actually aid in weight management and improve heart health. Avocados, with their creamy texture and mild flavor, are an excellent source of monounsaturated fats. They can be sliced atop salads, blended into smoothies, or mashed into guacamole, offering versatility and richness to meals.

Nuts and seeds, including almonds, walnuts, chia seeds, and flaxseeds, provide a concentrated source of healthy fats, fiber, and protein. They make for a convenient snack or a delightful addition to salads and baked goods. A handful of almonds or a sprinkle of chia seeds in your morning yogurt can enhance both flavor and nutrition.

Olive oil, a staple of the Mediterranean diet, is renowned for its health benefits. It's rich in antioxidants and monounsaturated fats, which have been linked to reduced risk of chronic diseases. Use olive oil as a base for salad dressings, for sautéing vegetables, or as a finishing touch on roasted dishes. Its fruity aroma and subtle flavor can elevate simple ingredients to gourmet status.

Incorporating lean proteins and healthy fats into your diet doesn't require drastic changes but rather thoughtful substitutions and additions. Start by replacing fatty cuts of meat with leaner options, such as swapping ground beef for ground turkey or choosing fish over pork. Introduce more plant-based proteins into your meals, perhaps by having a meatless day each week, focusing on legumes and tofu.

When it comes to fats, opt for sources that provide nutritional benefits beyond calories. Replace butter and margarine with olive oil or avocado oil in your cooking. Snack on a small handful of nuts instead of processed chips or crackers. These small changes can have a significant impact on your overall health and well-being.

Meal preparation can also play a key role in integrating these nutrient-dense foods into your lifestyle. Plan your meals around lean proteins and healthy fats, ensuring that each dish is balanced and nourishing. For instance, a dinner of grilled chicken, quinoa, and a side of roasted vegetables drizzled with olive oil offers a harmonious blend of protein, healthy fats, and complex carbohydrates.

As you explore the world of lean proteins and healthy fats, remember that balance and variety are key. By incorporating a wide range of these foods into your diet, you not only support your health but also keep meals exciting and enjoyable. Think of each meal as an opportunity to nourish your body, providing it with the essential nutrients it needs to thrive.

In the end, the journey toward incorporating lean proteins and healthy fats into your diet is one of discovery and empowerment. It's about making informed choices that align with your health goals and personal preferences. Embrace the abundance of nature's offerings, savor the flavors and textures, and enjoy the vitality that comes with nourishing your body the right way.

One-pot and Sheet Pan Meals

Cooking can sometimes feel like a juggling act, especially when time is scarce or energy wanes at the end of a long day. Enter the world of one-pot and sheet pan meals, offering simplicity and efficiency without sacrificing flavor. These cooking methods streamline meal preparation by minimizing the number of dishes used, making them ideal for busy individuals or anyone seeking to simplify their culinary routine.

One-pot meals conjure images of hearty stews, comforting pastas, and aromatic curries, all simmering away in a single vessel. The magic of these meals lies in the way flavors meld together, creating depth and complexity with minimal effort. Imagine a pot on the stove, filled with onions, garlic, and bell peppers sautéing to perfection. Add chunks of chicken, a handful of spices, and a splash of broth, allowing everything to cook together, the ingredients infusing one another with their unique flavors. The result is a dish that's rich, satisfying, and surprisingly easy to prepare.

A classic example of a one-pot wonder is the humble risotto. Start by gently cooking onions and garlic in olive oil until fragrant. Stir in Arborio rice, letting it toast slightly before gradually adding warm broth, ladle by ladle. Stir continuously, coaxing the starches out of the rice, creating a creamy texture. As the rice nears doneness, fold in fresh peas, lemon zest, and a sprinkle of Parmesan cheese. The risotto is ready when the rice is tender yet retains a slight bite, each grain enveloped in a luxurious, velvety sauce. This dish illustrates the beauty of one-pot cooking, where simple ingredients transform into an elegant meal.

Chili is another one-pot favorite, perfect for feeding a crowd or preparing in advance for busy nights. Begin by browning ground beef or turkey in a large pot, then add onions, garlic, and bell peppers, cooking until softened. Introduce canned tomatoes, kidney beans, and a medley of spices—cumin, paprika, and chili powder—stirring everything together. Let the chili simmer gently, allowing the flavors to marry and develop depth. Serve it with warm cornbread or a dollop of sour cream for a cozy, satisfying meal.

Similarly, sheet pan meals offer the convenience of cooking an entire meal on a single tray, allowing the oven to do most of the work. The concept is simple: arrange protein, vegetables, and seasonings on a baking sheet, then roast until everything is cooked through and caramelized. This method not only saves time but also encourages the natural flavors of the ingredients to shine.

Consider a sheet pan of roasted vegetables and salmon. Arrange cherry tomatoes, bell peppers, and zucchini on a baking sheet, drizzling with olive oil and seasoning with salt, pepper, and thyme. Nestle salmon fillets amidst the vegetables, giving them a light brush of Dijon mustard for flavor. Roast in a hot oven until the fish is cooked and the vegetables are tender and slightly charred. The result is a meal that's vibrant, healthy, and full of flavor—a testament to the power of sheet pan cooking.

Another delightful sheet pan creation is chicken fajitas. Toss sliced bell peppers and onions with strips of chicken breast, olive oil, and a blend of spices like cumin and paprika. Spread the mixture on a sheet pan and roast until the chicken is cooked through and the vegetables are caramelized. Serve with warm tortillas, avocado, and lime wedges for a meal that's as festive as it is convenient.

For those new to one-pot and sheet pan meals, the key is to experiment with different ingredients and flavor combinations. Start with simple recipes, gradually exploring more complex dishes as confidence grows. Pay attention to cooking times and temperatures, ensuring that proteins and vegetables are cooked to perfection. The beauty of these meals is their adaptability—feel free to swap ingredients based on personal preference or seasonal availability.

In addition to their convenience, one-pot and sheet pan meals offer the added benefit of streamlined cleanup. With fewer dishes to wash, you can spend more time enjoying your meal and less time scrubbing pots and pans. This simplicity extends beyond the cooking process, encouraging a more relaxed and enjoyable dining experience.

To make the most of these cooking methods, invest in quality cookware and bakeware. A sturdy Dutch oven or a well-seasoned cast-iron skillet can be invaluable for one-pot meals, while a durable sheet pan ensures even roasting and easy cleanup. These tools will serve you well, becoming trusted companions in your culinary adventures.

One-pot and sheet pan meals also lend themselves to meal prepping and batch cooking. Prepare larger quantities, storing leftovers in the fridge or freezer for future meals. This approach not only saves time but also reduces food waste, as you can easily repurpose ingredients or dishes throughout the week.

Incorporating these meals into your routine can transform the way you approach cooking, offering a practical solution to the challenges of modern life. By embracing the simplicity and versatility of one-pot and sheet pan meals, you can enjoy delicious, home-cooked dinners with minimal fuss. The possibilities are endless, limited only by your imagination and willingness to explore new flavors and techniques. Savor the satisfaction that comes from creating nourishing meals with ease, and relish the time saved for the moments that truly matter.

Transforming Leftovers into New Dishes

Leftovers, often overlooked or discarded, hold untapped potential to be transformed into delightful new dishes. With a dash of creativity and a sprinkle of resourcefulness, yesterday's meals can become the foundation for today's culinary masterpieces. Embracing this approach not only reduces food waste but also offers convenience and cost savings while expanding your culinary repertoire.

Consider the humble roast chicken. After enjoying it as a centerpiece of a meal, the remnants can be repurposed in a myriad of ways. Strip the meat from the bones, reserving it for a comforting chicken soup. Simmer the carcass with onions, carrots, and celery to create a rich, flavorful broth. Add noodles, herbs, and the reserved chicken for a soup that warms the soul and satisfies the appetite. This transformation highlights the versatility of leftovers, turning them into a dish that's both nourishing and familiar.

Rice, a staple in many households, often finds itself languishing in the refrigerator after a meal. However, its potential goes far beyond a simple side dish. Day-old rice is perfect for making fried rice, a quick and satisfying meal that welcomes an array of ingredients. Sauté garlic and ginger in a hot pan, adding vegetables like peas, carrots, and bell peppers. Toss in the rice, breaking up any clumps, and stir in soy sauce and sesame oil for flavor. Incorporate scrambled eggs or tofu for protein, finishing with a sprinkle of green onions. This dish not only rejuvenates leftover rice but also allows for customization based on what's available in your pantry.

Pasta, another common leftover, can be given new life with a few thoughtful additions. If you find yourself with a surplus of cooked pasta, consider turning it into a savory frittata. Whisk together eggs, milk, and cheese, then fold in the pasta along with any vegetables or meats you have on hand. Pour the mixture into a heated, oven-safe skillet, cooking until the edges begin to set. Finish in the oven until the center is cooked through and the top is golden. Serve slices of this pasta frittata with a side salad for a meal that's as impressive as it is resourceful.

Vegetables, whether roasted, steamed, or sautéed, often make their way into the next day's meals with a bit of ingenuity. A medley of leftover vegetables can be transformed into a vibrant vegetable curry. Sauté onions, garlic, and ginger in coconut oil, adding curry powder and a touch of chili for heat. Stir in the vegetables, coating them in the fragrant spices, then pour in coconut milk and simmer until heated through. Serve this curry over rice or with naan for a dish that's both colorful and comforting.

For those with a sweet tooth, consider how dessert leftovers can be reinvented. Stale bread can be transformed into a luscious bread pudding. Cube the bread and soak it in a mixture of milk, eggs, sugar, and vanilla, allowing the flavors to meld. Bake until the pudding is set and golden, serving it warm with a drizzle of caramel or a scoop of ice cream. This transformation elevates simple ingredients into a dessert that feels indulgent and satisfying.

Repurposing leftovers also offers an opportunity to experiment with flavors and techniques you might not typically explore. Challenge yourself to think creatively about the ingredients at your disposal. Leftover grilled vegetables can become the star of a Mediterranean-inspired wrap, paired with hummus and feta cheese. Cold, cooked grains like quinoa or farro can be tossed with fresh herbs, lemon juice, and olive oil for a refreshing salad.

Meal planning with leftovers in mind can further enhance your efficiency in the kitchen. When preparing a meal, consider how the components might serve dual purposes. Roasting extra vegetables or cooking additional grains can provide the building blocks for future meals, reducing the need for additional cooking and preparation. This foresight not only saves time but also encourages mindful consumption, making the most of what you already have.

The possibilities for transforming leftovers are limited only by your imagination and willingness to experiment. Approach your refrigerator as a treasure trove of ingredients, each one a potential component of a new dish. By embracing the art of reinventing leftovers, you not only contribute to sustainability efforts but also hone your culinary skills.

Leftovers, often viewed as remnants of yesterday's meals, have the power to surprise and delight when given a chance. With a little creativity and a sense of adventure, you can transform these humble beginnings into dishes that are exciting and fulfilling. Enjoy the satisfaction that comes from making the most of your ingredients, and savor the unexpected pleasures that leftover transformations can bring to your table.

Healthy Alternatives to Processed Snacks

Navigating the aisles of any grocery store, it's easy to be overwhelmed by the sheer volume of processed snacks, all promising convenience and flavor. However, many of these treats are laden with unhealthy fats, sugars, and artificial ingredients. Finding healthy alternatives to these processed snacks can be both a rewarding and empowering experience, providing you with energy and nourishment without sacrificing taste. The journey to discovering such alternatives begins with understanding the basic principles of snacking wisely and making informed choices.

Whole foods, in their natural state, offer a plethora of options that can satisfy cravings while supporting overall health. Take, for instance, the humble apple. Crisp and refreshing, it's the perfect antidote to mid-afternoon hunger pangs. Pair it with a tablespoon of almond butter for added protein and healthy fats, creating a snack that not only satiates but also energizes. This combination is a testament to the power of whole foods, offering a balanced mix of carbohydrates, fats, and proteins in every bite.

Nuts and seeds are another fantastic alternative to reach for when the snack craving strikes. A small handful of almonds, walnuts, or sunflower seeds can provide a satisfying crunch while offering heart-healthy fats and a good source of fiber. These nutrient-dense snacks are easy to carry on-the-go and can be portioned out in advance to prevent overeating. For a touch of sweetness, consider adding dried fruits like apricots or raisins, but be mindful of portion sizes, as dried fruits can be higher in sugar.

For those who enjoy savory snacks, roasted chickpeas are an excellent choice. These legumes are packed with protein and fiber, making them a filling option. To prepare, toss canned or cooked chickpeas in olive oil and spices such as paprika, cumin, and garlic powder, then roast them in the oven until crispy. The result is a crunchy, flavorful snack that can rival any processed alternative.

Vegetable sticks paired with hummus or a yogurt-based dip provide a refreshing, crunchy snack that's both nutritious and satisfying. Carrot, cucumber, and bell pepper sticks offer a colorful array of vitamins and minerals, while hummus adds protein and healthy fats. This combination not only pleases the palate but also supports digestive health with its high fiber content. For a different twist, try making a dip with Greek yogurt, herbs, and lemon juice, offering a tangy, creamy accompaniment to the vegetables.

Popcorn, a classic snack, can be a healthy choice when prepared without excessive butter or salt. Air-popped popcorn is low in calories and high in fiber, making it an excellent option for those seeking a light snack. Enhance its flavor with a sprinkle of nutritional yeast for a cheesy taste or a dash of cinnamon for a hint of sweetness. This allows for a customizable snack that can cater to both savory and sweet cravings.

Smoothies serve as a versatile and nourishing snack, offering endless possibilities for customization. Start with a base of leafy greens like spinach or kale, adding a banana or a handful of berries for natural sweetness. Incorporate a protein source, such as Greek yogurt or a scoop of protein powder, to create a balanced and filling snack. The addition of flaxseeds or chia seeds can boost the nutrient content, providing omega-3 fatty acids and additional fiber. Blend with a liquid of choice, such as almond milk or coconut water, for a refreshing, nutrient-packed beverage that can be enjoyed any time of day.

For those who crave something more substantial, homemade energy bars or bites can be a satisfying alternative to store-bought varieties. Combine oats, nut butter, honey, and a selection of seeds or dried fruits, pressing the mixture into a pan or rolling it into balls. These can be stored in the refrigerator or freezer for easy access, offering a quick and convenient snack that's both wholesome and delicious.

Yogurt, particularly Greek yogurt, is an excellent option for those seeking a creamy, protein-rich snack. To avoid added sugars found in flavored varieties, opt for plain yogurt and enhance it with fresh fruits, a drizzle of honey, or a sprinkle of granola. This allows for control over the sweetness and adds a delightful texture contrast. For a savory twist, consider mixing in herbs and spices to create a yogurt dip, paired with whole-grain crackers or vegetable sticks.

Cottage cheese is another protein-packed option that can be enjoyed sweet or savory. Pair it with pineapple or berries for a touch of sweetness, or mix in cherry tomatoes and cucumbers for a refreshing, savory snack. Its versatility makes it a staple for anyone looking to incorporate more protein into their diet without resorting to processed options.

As you explore these healthy alternatives, remember that preparation and planning are key to successful snacking. Keep your pantry stocked with wholesome ingredients, making it easier to reach for nourishing options when hunger strikes.

Portion out snacks in advance, using reusable containers or bags, to ensure that you have convenient, ready-to-eat options on hand.

By embracing these alternatives to processed snacks, you have the opportunity to nourish your body while enjoying satisfying and flavorful options. The journey may require some adjustments and experimentation, but the rewards are well worth the effort. With each mindful choice, you take a step towards a healthier lifestyle, discovering the joy and satisfaction that comes from eating well. The vibrant flavors and textures of whole foods offer a delightful snacking experience, one that supports your health and well-being with every bite.

Nutritious Dips and Spreads

Gathering around a table with friends and family often involves a colorful array of dips and spreads, inviting everyone to indulge and share. These versatile creations add flavor and excitement to meals, transforming simple ingredients into delicious accompaniments. Nutritious dips and spreads can elevate snacks and meals while providing essential nutrients, making them a perfect addition to any kitchen repertoire. With a focus on healthful ingredients, these recipes offer endless possibilities for experimentation and enjoyment.

Hummus, a classic dip with roots in the Middle East, has become a staple in many households worldwide. Made from chickpeas, tahini, lemon juice, and garlic, it is a protein-rich and fiber-packed option that pairs well with an array of foods. The creamy texture and tangy flavor make it an ideal companion for fresh vegetables, whole-grain pita, or even as a spread on sandwiches and wraps. For a twist, try adding roasted red peppers, sun-dried tomatoes, or avocado to the basic recipe, creating variations that cater to different tastes and preferences.

Guacamole, a beloved dip originating from Mexico, is another nutritious option that brings a burst of flavor to the table. Composed of ripe avocados, lime juice, cilantro, and diced onions, guacamole is rich in heart-healthy monounsaturated fats and essential vitamins. Its creamy consistency and zesty taste make it a perfect match for tortilla chips, tacos, or as a topping for grilled proteins. To add depth and variety, consider incorporating ingredients like diced tomatoes, jalapeños, or even mango for a sweet and spicy twist.

For those seeking something lighter, tzatziki offers a refreshing alternative. This Greek dip combines creamy yogurt with cucumber, garlic, and dill, resulting in a cool and tangy accompaniment. Tzatziki is not only a delicious dip for fresh vegetables and warm pita but also serves as a flavorful sauce for grilled meats and falafel. The combination of protein-rich yogurt and hydrating cucumber makes it a nourishing option that can be enjoyed without guilt.

Nut and seed-based spreads provide another avenue for creating nutritious and satisfying additions to meals. Almond butter, for instance, offers a rich, nutty flavor along with a dose of healthy fats, protein, and vitamin E. Spread it on whole-grain toast, pair it with sliced apples, or incorporate it into smoothies for added creaminess. Similarly, sunflower seed butter provides a nut-free alternative with a similar nutritional profile, making it suitable for those with allergies.

Pesto, an Italian classic, can be reinvented in a multitude of ways to boost its nutritional value. Traditional pesto combines fresh basil, pine nuts, garlic, Parmesan cheese, and olive oil. However, experimenting with different greens, nuts, and cheese can yield exciting new flavors. Consider using kale or spinach as a base, walnuts or almonds instead of pine nuts, and nutritional yeast in place of cheese for a vegan option. Pesto can be stirred into pasta, spread on sandwiches, or used as a marinade for proteins.

Bean-based dips, such as black bean or white bean dip, offer another opportunity to incorporate nourishing ingredients into your diet. Pureed with olive oil, lemon juice, and spices, these dips provide a creamy texture and earthy flavor that complements a variety of foods. Serve them with vegetable sticks, whole-grain crackers, or as a filling for wraps and sandwiches. The high fiber and protein content of beans make these dips both satisfying and beneficial for digestive health.

Experimenting with different herbs and spices can further enhance the flavor and nutritional profile of dips and spreads. Incorporate turmeric, known for its anti-inflammatory properties, into hummus for a golden hue and earthy taste. Add a pinch of cayenne pepper to guacamole for an extra kick, or sprinkle smoked paprika over tzatziki for a hint of smokiness. These small additions can transform a familiar recipe into something new and exciting.

Creating homemade dips and spreads allows for control over the ingredients, ensuring that they are free from preservatives and excess sodium often found in store-bought versions. Preparing them at home also offers the opportunity to adjust flavors to suit personal preferences, whether you prefer a hint of garlic, a squeeze of lemon, or a dash of spice.

Incorporating these nutritious options into your meals can be as simple as keeping a few staple ingredients on hand. Stock your pantry with canned beans, nuts, and seeds, and ensure your refrigerator is filled with fresh herbs, lemons, and a variety of vegetables. This preparation makes it easy to whip up a dip or spread at a moment's notice, ensuring you always have a healthy option available.

The versatility of dips and spreads means they can be enjoyed in a multitude of ways, from a simple snack to a key component of a meal. They encourage creativity and exploration in the kitchen, allowing you to experiment with flavors and textures while providing nourishing benefits. By embracing these delicious and healthful options, you can enhance your culinary experiences and support a balanced diet, all while indulging in the joy of sharing food with others.

Sweet Treats with a Healthy Twist

Indulging in a sweet treat doesn't have to mean compromising on health. With a little creativity and the right ingredients, it's possible to enjoy desserts that are both delicious and nourishing. Sweet treats with a healthy twist offer the best of both worlds, satisfying cravings while providing beneficial nutrients. Whether you're baking at home or looking for quick fixes, there are countless ways to create desserts that bring joy and wellness together.

Consider the classic chocolate brownie, often regarded as a guilty pleasure. By substituting traditional ingredients with healthier alternatives, this beloved dessert can become a guilt-free indulgence. Swap out all-purpose flour for almond flour, adding a dose of protein and healthy fats. Replace sugar with natural sweeteners like maple syrup or ripe bananas, which not only reduce the glycemic load but also add moisture and depth of flavor. Incorporate dark chocolate or cocoa powder rich in antioxidants, and add a handful of walnuts for a satisfying crunch and additional nutrients. The result is a brownie that retains its rich, fudgy texture and chocolatey goodness while offering a healthier profile.

For those who enjoy fruit-based desserts, a simple berry crumble can be transformed into a nourishing treat. Use a mix of fresh or frozen berries, such as blueberries, raspberries, and strawberries, as the base. These fruits are packed with vitamins, fiber, and antioxidants, making them a vibrant and healthful choice. Create a crumble topping with oats, almond flour, and a touch of coconut oil, adding cinnamon for warmth and sweetness. Bake until the berries are bubbling and the topping is golden, serving it warm with a dollop of Greek yogurt or a scoop of dairy-free ice cream. This dessert not only highlights the natural sweetness of the berries but also provides a comforting and satisfying experience.

For a tropical twist, consider making a coconut chia pudding. Chia seeds, known for their high fiber and omega-3 content, create a creamy texture when soaked in liquid. Combine them with coconut milk and a dash of vanilla extract, letting the mixture sit overnight in the refrigerator. By morning, the chia seeds will have absorbed the liquid, resulting in a thick, pudding-like consistency. Top with sliced mango, pineapple, or kiwi for a burst of color and flavor. This refreshing dessert can be enjoyed as a guilt-free breakfast treat or a light, satisfying dessert.

Another delightful option is to make avocado chocolate mousse, a creamy and decadent dessert that surprises with its main ingredient. Avocado provides a smooth, silky texture and is rich in healthy fats and vitamins. Blend ripe avocados with cocoa powder, a splash of almond milk, and a natural sweetener like honey or agave syrup. The result is a luscious, chocolatey mousse that feels indulgent yet provides wholesome nutrients. Serve it chilled with a sprinkle of cacao nibs or fresh berries for an added touch.

For cookie lovers, oatmeal raisin cookies offer a wholesome alternative to traditional chocolate chip varieties. Use rolled oats as the base, adding almond flour for texture and natural sweetness. Incorporate mashed bananas or applesauce as a binder, reducing the need for additional fats or sugars. Mix in plump raisins, a dash of cinnamon, and a handful of chopped nuts for flavor and crunch. These cookies are not only easy to make but also provide a satisfying snack or dessert that can be enjoyed any time of day.

Ice cream, often considered a decadent treat, can also be reinvented with health in mind. Banana-based "nice cream" is a simple and nutritious alternative that requires just a few ingredients. Freeze ripe bananas, then blend them until smooth, creating a creamy, ice cream-like texture. Add flavors like vanilla, cocoa powder, or peanut butter for variety, and fold in mix-ins like chocolate chips or nuts for added interest. This frozen treat is not only dairy-free but also naturally sweetened, making it a perfect choice for those seeking a lighter dessert.

For those who cherish the flavors of autumn, a spiced apple crisp provides warmth and comfort. Slice apples, tossing them with cinnamon, nutmeg, and a touch of maple syrup. Arrange them in a baking dish and top with a mixture of oats, almond flour, and pecans, drizzled with coconut oil. Bake until the apples are tender and the topping is crisp and golden. Serve warm with a scoop of yogurt or a drizzle of almond butter for a cozy, satisfying dessert that embraces the season's bounty.

Incorporating vegetables into desserts may seem unconventional, but it's a clever way to boost nutrition while enjoying a sweet treat. Zucchini bread, for example, uses shredded zucchini to add moisture and nutrients to a classic loaf. Combine it with almond flour, a touch of honey or maple syrup, and spices like cinnamon and nutmeg for a fragrant and flavorful bread. This versatile treat can be enjoyed as a snack, dessert, or even breakfast, offering a delicious way to sneak in some extra veggies.

Exploring these healthy twists on sweet treats not only satisfies a sweet tooth but also encourages a more mindful approach to eating. By choosing wholesome ingredients and experimenting with flavors, it's possible to enjoy desserts that align with a balanced lifestyle. With each bite, there's an opportunity to nourish the body and delight the senses, proving that indulgence and health can coexist harmoniously. The joy of creating and sharing these treats brings warmth and connection, making every moment a little sweeter.

Savory Munchies and Crunchies

Crunchy, savory snacks have a unique ability to satisfy cravings, offering texture and flavor that delight the senses. While many store-bought options are laden with unhealthy fats and excessive sodium, creating homemade versions allows for healthier alternatives without compromising on taste. By using wholesome ingredients and simple techniques, these savory munchies and crunchies can become a staple in your snack repertoire, providing nourishment and satisfaction in every bite.

One of the most beloved savory snacks is the classic roasted chickpea. These tiny legumes transform into a crunchy delight when tossed with olive oil and spices, then roasted until golden. Start with canned or cooked chickpeas, ensuring they are well-drained and patted dry. This step is crucial for achieving the desired crispiness. Season them with your choice of spices—cumin, paprika, garlic powder, or even a hint of cayenne for a kick. Spread them evenly on a baking sheet and roast until they reach a satisfying crunch. These roasted chickpeas are not only delicious but also packed with protein and fiber, making them a nutritious choice for any time of day.

For those who enjoy a touch of heat, spiced nuts provide a tantalizing option. Almonds, cashews, or pecans can be transformed into a savory snack with the right seasoning blend. Begin by toasting the nuts lightly in a dry pan to enhance their natural flavors. Then, toss them with a mixture of spices such as smoked paprika, chili powder, and a touch of sea salt. For a hint of sweetness, add a drizzle of maple syrup or honey, creating a balance that complements the heat. Roast the seasoned nuts in the oven until they are fragrant and crunchy, perfect for enjoying on their own or as an accompaniment to a cheese board.

Vegetable chips offer a healthy alternative to traditional potato chips, providing the same satisfying crunch without the guilt. Kale, sweet potatoes, and beets are excellent candidates for this transformation. For kale chips, wash and thoroughly dry the leaves, removing the tough stems. Toss them with a bit of olive oil and a sprinkle of sea salt, then bake until crisp. The result is a light, airy chip that retains the vibrant green hue of the kale. Sweet potato and beet chips can be made by slicing the vegetables thinly, either with a mandoline or a sharp knife. Season with olive oil and your choice of spices before baking until crispy. These colorful chips not only offer a variety of nutrients but also add visual appeal to any snack spread.

Popcorn, a timeless favorite, can be elevated with savory seasonings to create a gourmet snack. Air-pop a batch of popcorn, then toss it with olive oil or melted coconut oil to help the seasonings adhere. A sprinkle of nutritional yeast adds a cheesy flavor without dairy, while herbs like rosemary or thyme impart a fragrant aroma. For a spicy twist, consider adding chili powder or smoked paprika. The options are endless, and popcorn's versatility makes it a canvas for creativity.

For a fusion of flavors, consider making savory granola. While granola is typically associated with sweet breakfasts, a savory version can be a delightful surprise. Combine rolled oats with seeds such as pumpkin or sunflower, adding nuts like almonds or walnuts for texture. Season with olive oil, soy sauce, and spices like garlic powder and smoked paprika. Bake until golden, stirring occasionally to ensure even toasting. This savory granola can be enjoyed as a crunchy topping for salads or soups, or as a stand-alone snack.

Cheese straws are another savory delight that combines the richness of cheese with the crispness of pastry. Using puff pastry as a base, roll it out and sprinkle generously with grated cheddar or Parmesan cheese, along with a touch of cayenne pepper for heat. Cut the pastry into strips, twist them, and bake until they are puffed and golden. These cheese straws are perfect for parties or as an accompaniment to a bowl of soup.

For a Middle Eastern-inspired snack, try making za'atar pita chips. Cut whole-grain pita bread into triangles and brush them with olive oil. Sprinkle with za'atar, a fragrant blend of herbs and spices including thyme, sesame seeds, and sumac. Bake until crisp and serve with hummus or baba ghanoush for a taste of the Mediterranean.

Homemade crackers offer another opportunity to create a crunchy, savory snack tailored to your preferences. Combine whole grain or almond flour with seeds like flax or sesame, adding water and olive oil to form a dough. Roll the dough thin, cut into shapes, and bake until golden. Season with herbs, spices, or even grated cheese for added flavor. These crackers are a wholesome alternative to store-bought versions and can be customized with various toppings.

Exploring these savory munchies and crunchies not only satisfies the craving for something salty and crunchy but also encourages a more mindful approach to snacking. By choosing quality ingredients and experimenting with flavors, it's possible to enjoy snacks that align with a balanced lifestyle. Each bite offers an opportunity to nourish the body and delight the senses, demonstrating that homemade snacks can be both indulgent and health-conscious. With a little creativity and experimentation, these savory treats can become a cherished part of your culinary repertoire, bringing joy and satisfaction to every snacking occasion.

On-the-go Snack Solutions

In today's fast-paced world, finding time to prepare and enjoy nutritious snacks can be a challenge. Whether you're commuting, traveling, or simply running errands, the need for convenient, portable snacks is undeniable. On-the-go snack solutions offer a way to maintain energy levels and satisfy hunger without resorting to unhealthy options. By planning ahead and choosing wisely, it's possible to enjoy snacks that are both convenient and nourishing, keeping you fueled throughout your busy day.

A key component of successful on-the-go snacking is preparation. By dedicating a small amount of time each week to snack prep, you can ensure that wholesome options are readily available when you need them. Start by identifying snacks that are easy to transport and have a longer shelf life. Nuts and seeds, for example, are excellent choices. Almonds, walnuts, and sunflower seeds provide a good source of protein, healthy fats, and fiber, making them a satisfying option for any time of day. Portion them into small, reusable containers or bags, and keep them in your bag or car for easy access.

Another convenient snack solution is the homemade energy bar or ball. These snacks are simple to prepare and can be customized to fit your taste preferences and dietary needs. Combine oats, nut butter, and honey or maple syrup as a base, then add ingredients like seeds, dried fruit, or dark chocolate chips for extra flavor and nutrition. Press the mixture into a pan to create bars or roll it into balls, then store them in the refrigerator or freezer. These energy-packed snacks are perfect for a quick boost during a busy day.

For those who prefer savory snacks, roasted chickpeas or edamame offer a crunchy and nutritious option. Both are rich in protein and fiber, providing a satisfying alternative to traditional chips or crackers. To prepare roasted chickpeas, toss canned or cooked chickpeas with olive oil and your choice of spices, then roast them in the oven until crispy. Similarly, edamame can be seasoned with sea salt or chili powder and roasted for an added crunch. These snacks can be stored in airtight containers, making them easy to grab and go.

Fruits and vegetables are also excellent on-the-go snack options, offering natural sweetness and essential vitamins. Choose fruits that are sturdy and don't require peeling, such as apples, bananas, or grapes. For vegetables, consider packing carrot sticks, cherry tomatoes, or cucumber slices. Pair them with a small container of hummus or a yogurt-based dip for added flavor and satisfaction. These snacks not only provide hydration and nutrients but also help curb cravings for less healthy options.

Yogurt, particularly Greek yogurt, is another portable snack that offers a good source of protein and probiotics. To make it travel-friendly, opt for single-serving containers or transfer yogurt into a reusable jar. Top it with fresh berries, nuts, or a sprinkle of granola for added texture and flavor. This combination makes for a balanced and satisfying snack that can be enjoyed at any time.

Whole-grain crackers or rice cakes can also be part of a convenient snack solution. Pair them with a small packet of nut butter or a slice of cheese for a satisfying combination of carbohydrates, protein, and healthy fats. These snacks are easy to pack and can be enjoyed without the need for utensils, making them ideal for eating on the go.

For those who enjoy baking, homemade muffins or bread can be a versatile snack option. Choose recipes that incorporate whole grains, fruits, or vegetables to boost the nutritional value. For instance, banana or zucchini muffins provide natural sweetness and moisture, while whole-grain bread with seeds offers a hearty texture. Bake them in advance and store them in the freezer, then grab a portion when you need a quick snack.

Smoothies, while typically enjoyed at home, can also be transformed into a portable snack with the right container. Blend a combination of fruits, vegetables, and a protein source like yogurt or protein powder, then pour the mixture into a leak-proof bottle. Consider adding flaxseeds or chia seeds for additional fiber and omega-3 fatty acids. A well-prepared smoothie offers a refreshing and nutrient-dense snack that can be sipped throughout the day.

As you explore these on-the-go snack solutions, it's important to consider your personal preferences and dietary needs. Experiment with different combinations and flavors to find snacks that you enjoy and that fit your lifestyle. Keep a variety of options on hand to prevent boredom and ensure that you always have a healthy choice available.

The key to successful on-the-go snacking lies in preparation and mindfulness. By planning ahead and choosing nutrient-dense options, you can maintain energy levels and stay satisfied, no matter where your day takes you. With a little creativity and effort, it's possible to enjoy snacks that support a balanced diet while fitting seamlessly into your busy schedule. Embrace the convenience of these portable snacks and discover the joy of nourishing your body, even when time is limited.